D1479524

The Financial Times Book of Garden Design

The Financial Times Book of Garden Design

EDITOR Anthony Huxley

CONTRIBUTORS John Brookes, Robin Lane Fox, Arthur Hellyer MBE, FLS, VMH, AHRHS

DAVID & CHARLES

Newton Abbot · London · Vancouver

0 7153 67773

Set in Monotype Univers
and printed in Great Britain
by Tinling (1973) Limited Prescot Merseyside
for David & Charles (Holdings) Limited
South Devon House Newton Abbot Devon

Designed by John Leath

Contents

Foreword

by the EARL OF DROGHEDA, Chairman, The Financial Times Ltd

It was in 1970 that the *Financial Times* first decided to have an outdoor garden at the Chelsea Flower Show. We felt that it would be a helpful promotional exercise for demonstrating to the large number of people who visited Chelsea each year that the *Financial Times* was not simply interested in money and business but ranged much further afield. We were already running two weekly gardening articles, one by one of the 'grand old men' of gardening, Arthur Hellyer, whose all-round experience and knowledge is second to none; and the other by a brilliant young historian and gardening expert, Robin Lane Fox, whose splendid contributions to the paper were giving regular proof that gardening was also a hobby for young people.

Having decided to venture upon a garden at the Chelsea Flower Show there came the question of whether or not we could afford it. To our great delight we discovered that no rental whatsoever was charged for the space occupied by the garden and that costs were simply confined to the actual construction work and the subsequent restoration of the garden. Both Arthur Hellyer and Robin Lane Fox felt that the services of a qualified landscape architect must be engaged in order that the various ideas could be co-ordinated and clearly interpreted in working drawings. Accordingly, the well-known designer John Brookes was approached and happily he undertook to become a member of the team. We also engaged the services of Gavin Jones Nurseries, the head of which, Mr Geoffrey Chalk, had had many years of experience in the construction and planning of gardens. Thus the team was complete.

The first garden, which was a design for a simple town garden, met with the approval of the judges and won a gold medal. Its success (despite atrocious weather) made us feel that we should have another go and so, with the same team working together, we presented another garden at the 1972 Chelsea Flower Show and this, too, won a gold medal. The question then was whether we should carry on and we decided to have a third try, on this occasion in association with Exbury Gardens Limited who gave us immense help and to whom we are profoundly grateful for their invaluable assistance both with plants and with advice.

Opinion must differ as to which of the three gardens was the most effective. I personally liked the third best but all three had great merit and all three met with the approval of the stern judges of the Royal Horticultural Society. During the third year costs had mounted considerably and we felt that if we were to continue for a fourth year we might find ourselves well into the five-figure range and also we might be tempting providence in seeking after yet another gold medal. We therefore decided to rest upon our laurels (no joke intended) and to desist from further enterprises for the time being.

Before the presentation of the 1973 garden the gardening world was impoverished through the death of Geoffrey Chalk, and if the *Financial Times* returns to Chelsea, which I greatly hope we shall do, we shall seriously miss the presence of our splendid friend and colleague.

Foreword

by LORD ABERCONWAY, President, The Royal Horticultural Society

No garden, however fine, can stand still. The plants in a garden grow, jostle, and fight for space; and so the garden changes, perhaps for the better as the plants mature, perhaps for the worse, if they are not spaced out and the garden is not in other ways properly cultivated. But there can be a 'moment of truth' when a garden, for an instant of time, may be seen as an ideal. A garden created as a temporary work of art 'à point' can be a thing of great, and natural, beauty.

So it was with the three highly individual gardens, each outstandingly successful in design and execution, which the *Financial Times* created at Chelsea in 1971, 1972 and 1973, to the pleasure of The Royal Horticultural Society, and to the enjoyment of its Fellows and the public who saw them. And though the beauty of such a transient garden is not meant to last, its savour can be retained and preserved in descriptive prose: this is the object of this book, and it is achieved.

In forming these gardens, through its admirable and balanced team of experts to whom Lord Drogheda in his introduction pays tribute, the *Financial Times* did a fine service both to gardening and, as I believe, to itself, in showing the wide range of its interests.

My only regret, as President of the Royal Horticultural Society, is that Lord Drogheda confesses to a desire to rest upon his laurels. I console myself by the thought that the leaves of that plant, whether worn around the brow or placed beneath a resting body, soon become brittle, itchy and finally prickly. So I hope that so spurred again to action, and despite the ravages of inflation (the worst of all gardening pests), the *Financial Times* may before long bestir itself and make a garden again at the world's finest flower show.

Editor's preface

With introductions to this book by Lord Drogheda, chairman of the *Financial Times*, and Lord Aberconway, President of the Royal Horticultural Society, it may seem superfluous for the editor to add a preface. However, I wanted to record how much I have enjoyed working on the project with the three authors – one of whom, Arthur Hellyer, taught me so much of both gardening and editing during the many years I worked under him.

As Lord Drogheda's introduction explains, the three authors represent a remarkable, if not unique, combination of originality and experience. Despite its basis of the three Chelsea gardens, the book has a much wider purpose, focussing as it does on the making of attractive gardens despite the present problems of upkeep and often restricted space. And today, as John Brookes points out, the garden has to cater for a whole spectrum of needs, facilities and people of different ages apart from its basic qualities of decoration and restfulness.

As a designer, John is concerned with selecting plants appropriate to the site, rather than growing a large range of species jumbled together. This does not minimise the value of the many plant suggestions made by Robin Lane Fox, for they concentrate on structure, texture and mood in the context of carefully thought out groupings and contrasts. And though a very good gardener and plantsman himself, Arthur Hellyer has here subordinated his wider interests to the need to maintain the garden with minimum effort, combining well-tried methods with reasoned use of modern science and technology. Although relatively brief, like the other two sections, his is a model of concision, covering a wide range of topics.

I am proud to be associated with a volume which will, I hope, provide help and inspiration to gardeners in the present rather difficult times.

Part 1

Design

by John Brookes

Gardens which have survived from earlier centuries all seem to have a definite plan. Is this coincidence or is it because they have some bones in their layout, a basic discipline which has enabled them to be preserved in their original form? The plan may not necessarily have evolved on the drawing board. It would often have been beaten out through usage, location and site conditions over a period of time, giving the area an ageless quality of rightness for its situation and from this a restfulness seldom found in the modern garden. The result is as pleasing now as when it was created, because it has a recognisable form and function.

Such a design not only provides the right background for the people it serves but complements the style, materials and form of the house it adjoins, so that house and garden as well as the people using them work together as a unified whole. Within this disciplined framework, plants are deployed mainly to enhance and extend the basic plan; their ability to give pleasure, through colour, scent or texture, is of secondary importance. In any case, such individual qualities of plants, when not culinary or medicinal, are of fairly recent appeal.

It is surprising that the current manifestation of garden design is so dull. The eighteen-century landscape school has been called England's 'only true indigenous art form' and it is interesting to recall that at the time there was much public debate as to its relative merits – as realised in rolling parkland – in comparison with many of the formal layouts which its advent destroyed. It is difficult to appreciate that the curve – as a created line in garden design – was new then and therefore controversial. Until that time man had rejected the condition of wildness and had firmly mastered it into rigid garden patterns. Not until the eighteenth century did he take his inspirations from nature and natural forms, ultimately taming them to produce the typical park landscape of Kent, Brown and Repton. Today's gardens are often a bastard form of that precedent.

Cannot more inspiration be drawn from the shapes and contours of modern painting and sculpture to create a new concept of garden layout? A way has been shown by designers in California. In Brazil, Roberto Burle Marx produces exciting designs which marry horticulture to art forms, but what is right for South America will not transpose successfully to a gentler landscape. Gardens in Europe, whether public or private, are different again, as a visit to any of the biennial exhibitions will show. The modern Japanese garden – albeit an updated version of the traditional one – has moved on and is experimenting with new, both hard and soft, materials. In England, there are the plants and some of the most superb garden locations in the world with which to create a new form.

Over the last 100 years or so, garden layout has sadly deteriorated, not through lack of labour or money but from over-emphasis on a wide range of plant species. Layout has suffered at the expense of horticultural interest, especially in England, where so many imported foreign plants thrive in the favourable climate and are accepted as indigenous, so that gardeners have lost the capacity to decide what is right, while previously only what was right would grow. Now there is a wide selection of plants from China, Australasia, South Africa and the West Coast of the United States all existing side by side with the locals. No wonder the result is often a visual mess.

Hand in hand with a capacity to select plant material appropriate for the site is the need to appreciate the qualities of plants – or, conversely, to use only those which have more than one characteristic – for, as gardens become progressively smaller, the area available to specialist plants is necessarily limited. But the suitability of the plant to the garden is of less importance than the fitness of the garden to its owner. It is this aspect which has been overlooked for so long. The man who enjoys pottering in his garden at the weekend has until now been prepared to put up with its disadvantages – from the point

Town-garden layout plan. The pattern is formal although asymmetrical. There are cross balances over the pool between the specimen trees and the white bench seat, and the mixed border next to the terrace and the little vegetable garden at the far end. The garden is designed as though the terrace ran on from the house.

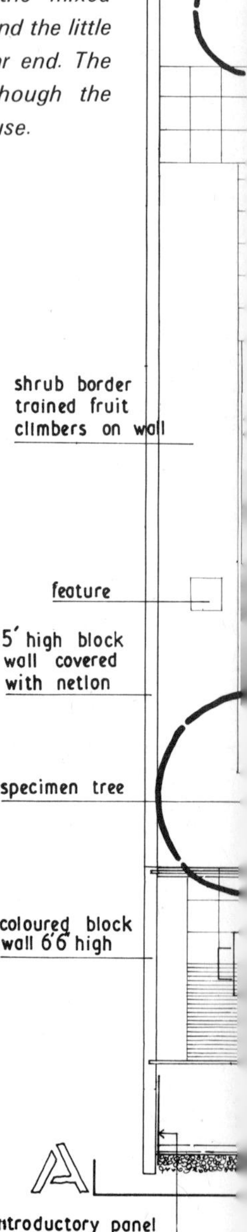

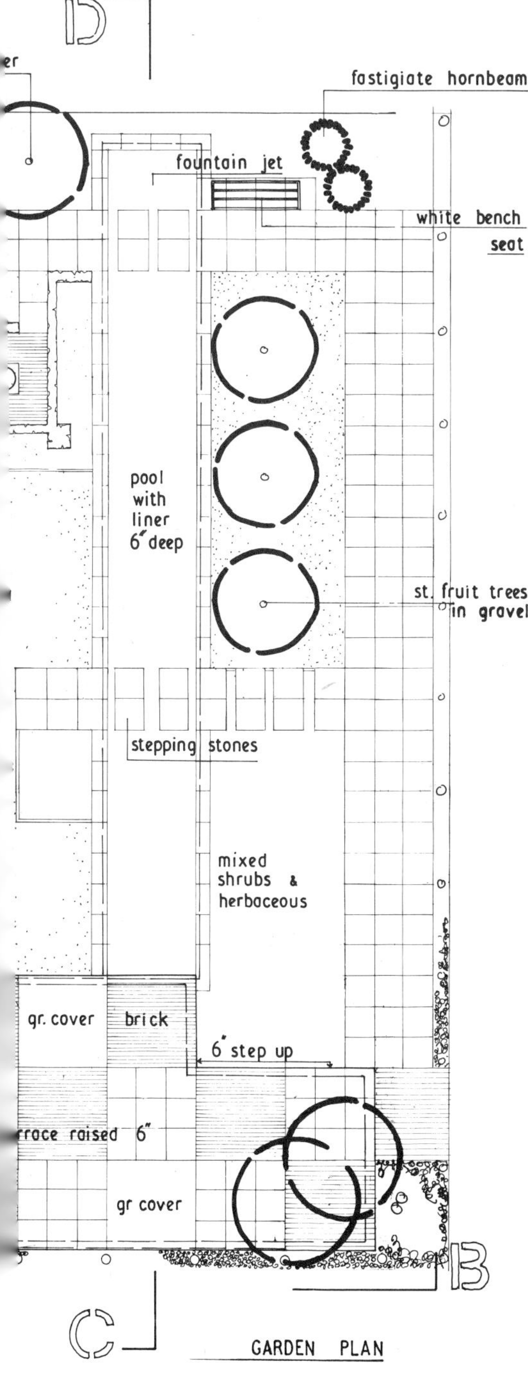

of view both of the user and of maintenance – and its increasing work load. But his horizons seem to be widening and, to meet the demands on his spare time, some form of rationalisation of the garden area seems more than ever essential.

Whether traditional or modern in design, the garden must cater for a whole spectrum of needs. It must serve not only as a place where the family can relax among colourful, scented planting, but as play space for children or recreational area for adults, perhaps with facilities for swimming, tennis or even a sauna. It may need to accommodate unobtrusive siting for cars, a boat or a caravan, as well as greenhouse, frames, oil storage tank, tool sheds and dust bins, at the same time allowing for easy usage of mechanical gadgets.

Design principles are the same for all gardens on whatever scale and in whatever location; it is their interpretation which differs, making each situation unique. The suburban garden, for instance, is a compromise between the principles of the town garden and the country garden; only the scale has altered.

The prime elements of all locations will be incorporated into one overall pattern, which is then rationalised into a garden and a usable extension of the home. The traditional symmetrical formal pattern is somewhat rigid for present-day needs; an asymmetric version of it is more practical. The free-shaped pattern is suitable for a country garden and a large suburban plot, while a modern or abstract layout can be adapted for a smaller garden. The design should be simple, but with a degree of subtlety if the end result is to achieve that essential rightness for its location which is the most admirable quality of the earlier gardens.

THE TOWN GARDEN

The town garden with which we are concerned occupies any small site enclosed by buildings or walls, or it might be a roof space. It could be in London, New York, Rome or any other residential area of comparable size anywhere in the world. Such a garden should be a retreat, a lung in the city. It is a green atmosphere that is aimed for, in spite of site restrictions. The area must be thought of on its own terms if the maximum satisfaction is to be derived from it.

The processes for designing a garden are the same in whatever location. First, before even putting spade to earth, clearly define for yourself what is wanted. The question is: how do you intend to use the area? In a family situation the immediate need will probably be for somewhere to stand the pram or where the children can play. If they are at the tricycle-riding stage, a hard circuit may be wanted, with ramps instead of steps. When considering the installation of a pool, either for plants or swimming, the positioning of the pump chamber and filtration must first be decided. The most likely use of such a restricted area, however, will probably be as a simple place for relaxation, where you can take a book or have a drink on a summer evening. It might be put to purely visual use, but even so there are twelve months of the year to bear in mind at the planning stage, as each plant must earn its keep the whole time. For our town garden at Chelsea the basic requirements were a terrace, some colour, some privacy, a place for herbs, the odd radish and some fruit, a compost heap and some water – fairly typical demands.

Having listed your working needs, you must next consider the character of the site and the materials you will use in the construction of the garden area. These are important elements in the design process. Old stock brick in a London courtyard, for example, has a different character from the stone in a similar

Left: *the terrace of the town garden at the Chelsea Flower Show. Blue bricks were used in areas to make up a chequer-board pattern with precast concrete slabs. The boundary wall is also of concrete block construction, capped with brick.*

A real town-garden situation which is virtually a backyard. Changes of level and overhead beams, later to be covered with climbers, keep the interest in the confined site. The structure under the window is to conceal dustbins.

situation in Edinburgh or Paris, while the red brick of old Washington is not the same as that used with flint in Winchester. The age of the house itself will also dictate the style of the garden, though perhaps more in the proportion of the layout than as a direct influence of an older period. The chances are that any attempt to recreate a historical design to complement a period house might not suit today's life style. Lip service can, however, be paid to an earlier style where a revamp of it will fulfil both physical and visual requirements. Topiary, for instance, which is mostly associated with cottage gardens or the medieval formal layout, can equally well be used in a modern plan – although formality need not mean pure symmetry. The finished result can still be one of equal balance while allowing for greater flexibility within the layout.

Today's style of garden, when well conceived and constructed, is as valid as that of any other period,

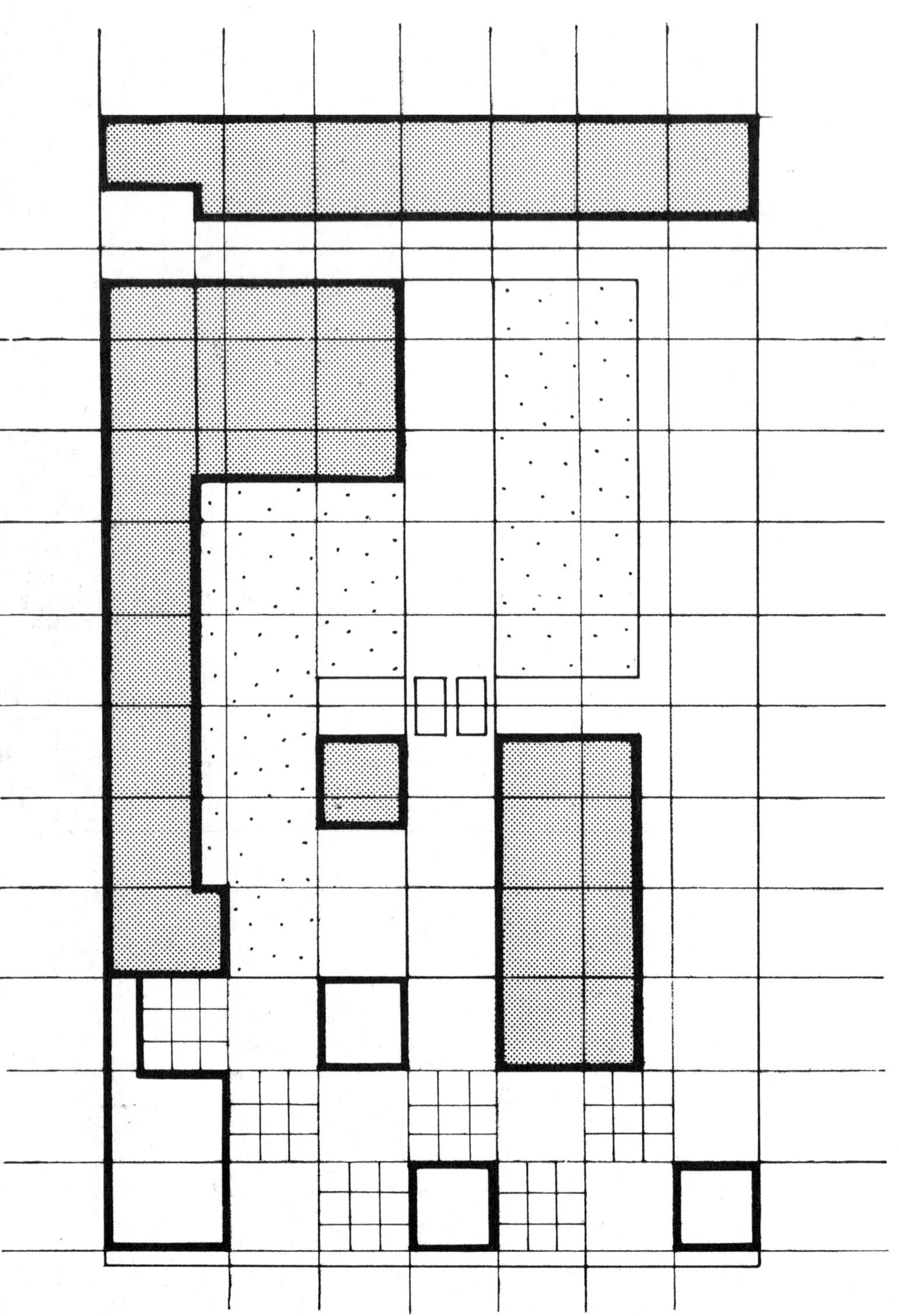

Right: *view over the country garden balustrading to the thatched garden room at the far end of the site. Plants are scattered among the gravel at the foot of the Versailles tubs to look as though the flowers had seeded themselves.*

The block plan of the town garden. Although the basic outlines are formal and symmetrical, internal divisions of planting are asymmetrical. The whole, however, achieves a very necessary balance.

The
Financial Times
town
garden

Left: *the town garden, designed as though the foreground terrace was directly in front of the house.*

The town garden in the course of construction. The central water canal, traversed by stepping stones, is lined with a plain-coloured polythene sheet. (Butyl rubber would have been used over a larger area.) Wide concrete slabs and no adjacent planting areas give ample opportunity to conceal and fix the sheeting.

Left: *the town garden had a strong disciplined design, but this was softened by planting. The foreground terrace is of squares of precast concrete paving and blue brickwork, interspersed with blocks of ground-cover planting.*

but it will only be crystallised as such if gardens are made for the people using them now. The planting and decoration must take second place to the fundamentals, for no amount of stocking or superfluous God-whattery will disguise a bad plan.

With the feel of the garden you want always in mind, start putting your ideas together. Site the working elements for their practical usage and interconnect them with hard surfacing. On a wet January morning, for instance, the distance between service access and dustbins is most important. Work first on paper and to a scale. Only in this way will you rationalise your ideal.

You are now assembling a sort of collage, inserting into the practical hard ground plan areas of lawn, gravel and planting. If you can work all these items into some sort of grid or proportionate pattern, they will hang together as one unit. This discipline is sound even though the plan may not be visible when

built, for the underlying logic will still read through. To give an analogy: a well-cut suit, no matter the material or colour, or what trimmings are later applied, will always be apparent; it will probably last well, too, since it is tailored to fit its wearer. The cut of garden depends on the guide lines into which you fit your pattern. Such a grid can often be worked out from the vertical piers of a garden wall or the range of windows in a building façade. With this framework you can fill in the different areas. The smaller the site, with proportionately more items to be included, the more important it is to have a logical system into which to fit them.

When exploring garden patterns in this way, it can be seen how the lines making up the plan – a wall, a step, a pointed tree – all contribute towards it. Lines, such as paths, running away from the house will tend to make the area appear longer; by narrowing these lines, you can even force a per-

The strong lines of pattern moving out from the foreground give the garden added visual length, but the pattern is stabilised by secondary lines at right angles, the rigid chequered pattern terrace area becoming more diffused.

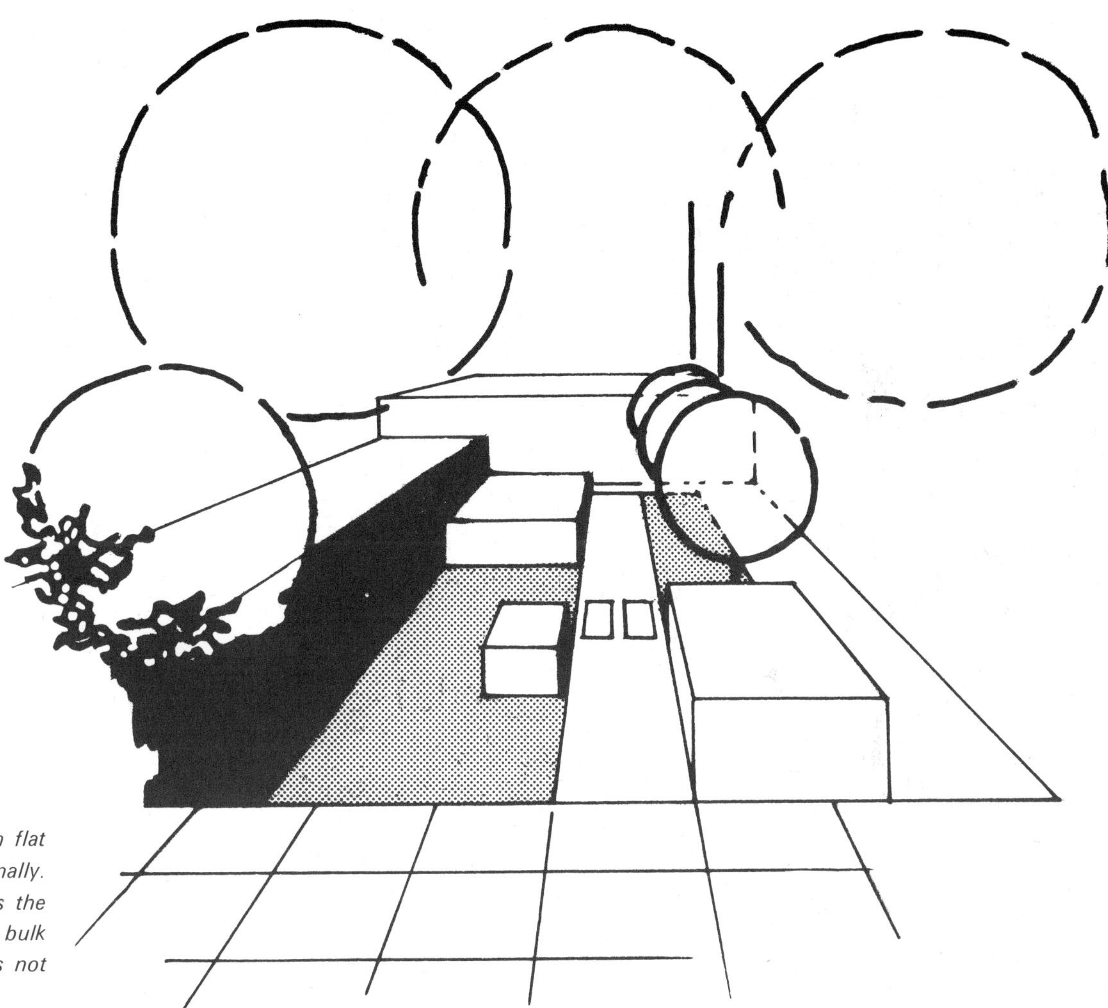

A garden design is not only conceived in flat plan but also considered three dimensionally. Space is moulded like sculpture – that is the bits between being as important as the bulk itself. At this stage the garden bulk does not need defining into plant forms.

spective to appear longer still. Lines running across the site tend to give it width.

In our town garden the usual divisions were broken down; hence fruit trees on one side of a long pond – which gave length to the garden – were counterbalanced by a little box-edged vegetable plot. Besides having edible products, both elements fitted naturally into the area. The water canal led the eye up the garden to the point where it disappeared among shadowy bamboo – this, if kept under control, looks marvellous in an urban setting.

When your own ground pattern seems to evolve almost as an abstract, start thinking about the area as masses and you will see that the voids between them are as important as the masses themselves. This then becomes a sculptural composition. What is so patently wrong with many gardens is that too much attention is given to the content of the masses, leaving the voids to look after themselves. The

result becomes piecemeal, with many slug-infested corners that are impractical to look after.

This is worth remembering in a small town garden where, with areas of paving, a strong ground pattern is often unavoidable. It is also necessary to hold the attention within the site; the tendency in a confined space is always to look up and out of it, and the eye should be anchored down.

You can now start to fill in the pattern. Take first the hard materials. For the fairly small town garden or courtyard quite expensive surfacing is worth considering. Slate is probably the most costly paving material away from its natural location. It is a hard substance, available in sizes similar to paving slabs and in a range of natural colours. It is well suited to roof gardens as it can be cut thin. In a modern setting it calls for a certain crispness of design. Old York stone is becoming increasingly difficult to obtain since there are now few public areas where such paving remains to be taken up and replaced

Loose gravel, retained by a brick-on-edge kerb, was the medium used for flooring our town garden. It contrasts well with brick paving, has a more urban quality than lawn and is splendid to sink pots into or to grow certain plants through. In short, for the town garden potterer it is ideal.

with concrete slabs. Old York should always be regular in outline. Crazy paving in this stone or in broken concrete slabs looks ragged unless extremely well laid, with individual pieces cut to fit together like a jigsaw.

Cut stone, another luxury material, appears somewhat ponderous and lacks the mellowness of old York, which has had the hard edges rubbed off. Brick is a wonderful flooring medium in most situations. It comes in a variety of colours and textures and has the advantage of running on to form useful kerbs. Standard bricks can be laid on edge, providing they are hard enough to withstand frost, or special paving bricks can be used which are quite thin but look like a standard brick when laid. Smooth brick tends to become slippery under trees, but a good scrub with a wire brush and salt will correct this. The terrace of our town garden was laid with a combination of brick on edge and concrete slabs. It was given a strong pattern of open planted squares alternating with the brick and paved squares on which tubs of lilies and other bulbs, annuals and scented-leaved geraniums could be set.

Concrete slabs, obtainable in numerous shapes, sizes, colours and textures, are today's major paving medium and not to be despised. They mellow quickly, are cheap and easy to lay and, used with subtlety, look very well indeed. Granite setts are a fine flooring material too, in a tough urban setting, but the surface is usually not smooth and they are better suited to infilling other hard surfaces to make a pattern. Cobbles can be laid in mortar or used loose to create a coarse gravel effect. Combinations of any of these paving materials can provide a most attractive surface. The end result should not, however, be loud; you are not flooring a pedestrian precinct but a quiet urban retreat.

Loose cobbles used as an infill between precast concrete paving slabs make a good contrast to bold leaf shapes, and also act as some sort of deterrent on corners.

Where small areas of grass are impracticable, paving and gravel make a particularly pleasing combination. Grass can become a muddy mess in town and also takes time to mow. So, in our garden, a general flooring of gravel was used throughout, with the odd plant straying into it as though self-seeded from the surrounding shrub borders. House plants, too, could be sunk into the gravel surface in summer, without looking too alien. When not used as a growing medium, the gravel surface can be sprayed with a weed-killer to prevent plants taking root; however, if it has been stabilised by rolling into hoggin (a mixture of clay and brick dust) possibly over ash, it will harden and weeds will not root into it. Only in loose gravel do weeds appear and, over a small area, these are easily removed by hand.

The lines of any changes of level should also fit into the overall grid pattern and are another way of helping to create ground interest. The same materials should be used for steps and retaining walls as have been selected for paving. Old York stone or concrete slabs, which do not lend themselves to walling, could cap a wall of brick, stone or concrete block.

When evolving a design, particularly for a small site, it is attention to detail which makes one layout better than another. With a little ingenuity, features can be arranged to serve a dual purpose so that the garden becomes less dotted with incident. For example, instead of a narrow flight of steps leading straight up and down between retaining walls, build wider treads where people can sit or pot plants can be set out; a conveniently sited retaining wall with a wide coping can be similarly used. Try turning a flight of steps so that the space beneath provides storage room for tools or a watering can.

In the town garden, the same ingenious ideas are needed as when planning a kitchen within an existing small space, so that every inch is made usable. The problem is very similar, for the garden design is basically that of an outside room, though furnished with plants. Such enclosed spaces can become extremely hot, so a shaded area will be needed in which to sit. Shade may be all too readily imposed by neighbouring houses, but where this is not the case some form of overhead beam or wire framework can be erected to support climbing plants or vines. It is important to sit in comfort out of

Old York stone and brick are an ideal combination for a period building. In this case lavender has seeded itself between paving joints making a random contrast to the furry grey leaves of Stachys lanata.

doors – a fact which manufacturers of metal garden furniture seem to have ignored. The garden is after all a place in which to relax. In European gardens there is always a corner set aside with comfortable seating, usually of a very unsophisticated nature and far removed from the ad man's dream! When planning this area, space can be allotted to a small barbecue, perhaps built in to double as an incinerator in the winter.

The sound of running water can bring a garden to life and has the added advantage in a built-up area of detracting from other less pleasant noise. The detailing of a pool should be carefully done, the area of water at ground level being fitted into the overall plan. Generally the simpler the shape and the larger the surface area the better; anything free-shaped, if not large enough, becomes niggardly and precious. If plastic or butyl sheeting is used to contain the pool, or a fibre-glass container, these must

In this town garden the awkward space under the metal stair has been cobbled and pots are set at the edge of it with lilies and agapanthus in them. The vine on the wall is Vitis coignetaie.

be well concealed; both have the disadvantage of lacking an outlet or overflow. A raised pool can be visually smaller; it provides a pleasant feature and is safer if children are about. Further, it avoids the necessity of excavation and the disposal of subsoil.

The limited amount of light or direct sunlight often prohibits a permanent colourful display in a town garden. Bright splashes of annual or bulb colour should therefore be reserved for tubs or pots grouped in the foreground and changed without too much expense during the season. In permanent shade there are many subjects which can be grown, tending to have fairly pale flowers or notable for their foliage alone. Rock plants are fairly difficult to maintain and generally have a short flowering time. In a small area, it is more rewarding to grow miniatures in a sink garden. A rockery is not an urban feature – to be attractive it should be of considerable size.

Above left: *the sort of casual seating arrangement under partial cover so enjoyable in a small town garden – in this case an exhibit by the General Trading Co Ltd of London at the Chelsea Flower Show.*

Pots can be bought in a wide range of materials, shapes and weights to suit most situations. The largest selection are on sale at garden centres where the buyer has the advantage of seeing them outside to gauge their suitability for his particular needs. The pots can be placed on shallow trays with castors so that they can be moved about easily to clear the deck for sunbathing or to accommodate extra chairs.

In an urban situation there is often a need to create a degree of privacy, not only from each side of the garden but from overhead as well. The overhang of a fine tree or the supports for climbing plants can at least baffle the viewer, though in a restricted space light will be taken from the house and sun excluded from the garden.

Nothing beats a good wall. It not only gives visual shelter but provides a noise barrier as well as a

Above: *a raised pool is much safer when children are about and provides an incidental feature to sit on for a drink or cup of coffee. The sound of running water can deaden neighbouring noises in a small space.*

Right: *where space is limited, pots can be set on shallow trays with castors, to be moved about at will.*

Privacy in town is often needed from above as well as from the sides. In this case white-painted timber beams have been used set on black scaffolding poles let into the old York stone paving. Climbers will eventually soften them. Note that the same timber dimension is used, although painted black, to heighten the surrounding brick wall to the garden.

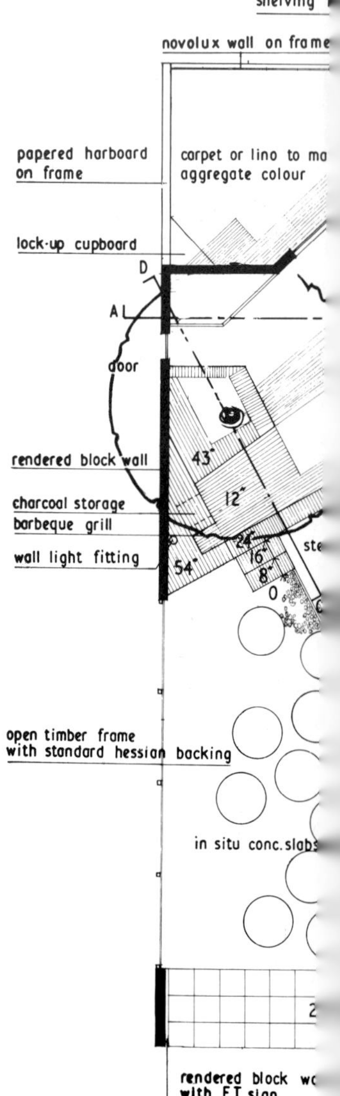

Below: *suburban-garden construction drawing. The line of the pool links back to the terrace and is broken by the random circular slabs which finish as a purely decorative feature in the pool. The design is fairly free but, nevertheless, balanced.*

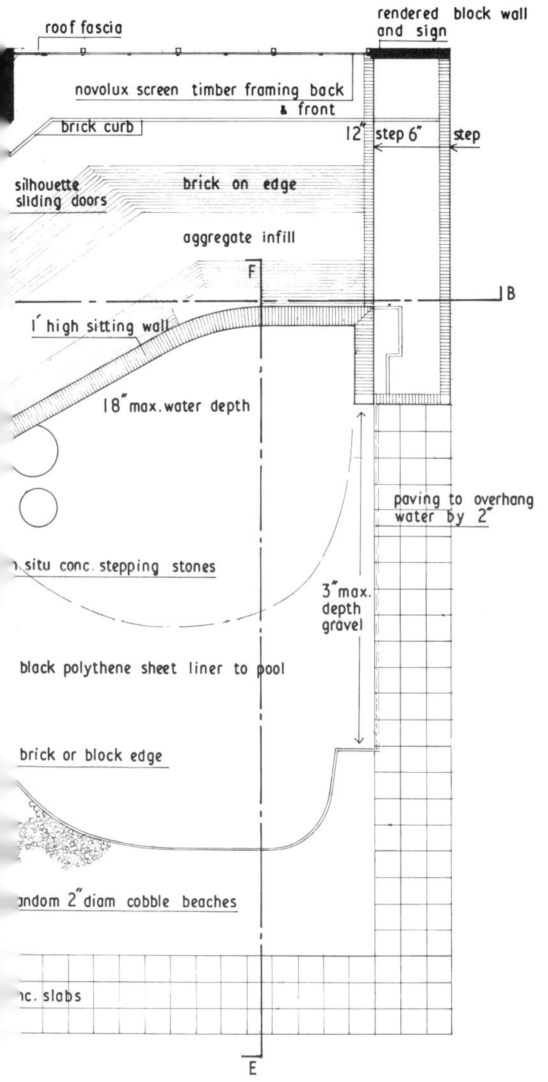

protected place where plants can be grown. The ideal is in brick 9in thick, though a cheaper version of 4in thickness has panels which overlap to provide a 9in pier at the necessary 8ft intervals. This technique can also be used with concrete blocks, a not unattractive alternative especially if coloured.

Though seldom tried, a solid boundary of asbestos panels within wooden frames can be built and then painted. Alternatively, opaque rigid vinyl sheeting, again within a framework, can be used, but the shiny surface will not hold self-clinging climbers. Timber fencing can give the necessary screen, though interwoven panelling seems thin and tends to rot quickly especially when entwined with vegetation. It is better to construct a fence with cedar or softwood treated with a preservative under pressure. Preservative stains are available in different colours.

To give height to an existing low wall, add one or two stout timber horizontals. Avoid the stock answer of trellis panels; while cheap to buy, they are quick to rot and invariably become entangled with the climber to which they started life as host.

When you have worked out the ground pattern, turn to planting. At this stage your concern is for background and skeleton planting to reinforce your basic plan and take it into the third dimension. A special tree of a particularly strong shape and sited like a piece of statuary might be a prominent feature to enliven the whole design. At the top of our Chelsea garden a specimen tree (*Robinia hispida*) was counter-positioned diagonally opposite a simple seat. Against your skeleton planting, the subjects of your choice can be grouped to achieve an interesting cycle of colour, texture and shape throughout the year.

To emphasise the feeling of retreat from urban pressures, the conservatory is making a reappearance. This is not the converted 'home extension' which always seems too hot in summer and too cold in winter, but the real thing. When properly tiled and heated, with the sound of splashing water or a canary singing, and masses of scented bulbs, winter living takes on a new dimension, even at the cost of losing valuable outdoor space. With correctly placed doors and plenty of ventilation, the conservatory in summer need not become a sweat box but an open arbour, giving shelter and privacy, and providing a marvellous refuge on a damp summer evening. A successful conservatory needs to have its functions clearly defined and its planting material chosen accordingly. It can all too easily become a storage overflow or, at the other extreme, a mixed exhibit of banked bloom. It should, like your garden, be a usable place with a congenial atmosphere, furnished with greenery.

The design of our town garden, then, was formal but asymmetric; not aspiring to grandeur but with a definite urban sophistication. It certainly embodied the most valuable virtue of all – that it should be no more difficult to maintain than you choose to make it.

THE SUBURBAN GARDEN

The dictionary defines a suburb as an outlying part of a city, and it is in this peripheral zone that there is the greatest concentration of gardens. The larger the garden the more desirable the property will be, yet the owner, fully occupied with other commitments, will probably have little time to look after it. This is where a good design – taking into account its drawbacks and exploiting its features – will prove an asset.

The average suburban house is comparatively new and likely to be inhabited by a younger family, so that more modern treatment is called for. The owner of such a house, with an automated kitchen, two cars and perhaps a boat on the river, can create whatever sort of world he wants with his garden, which should reflect his life style. He uses up-to-date furnishings in his house, so why not extend this practice outside? What is more there are new ways of using existing materials. The fundamental constituents of landscape – earth, water and vegetation – do not change, but they can be adapted to complement the man, his family and his home in a suburban setting.

To comply with just a situation, our garden design featured a patio area separated by sliding glass doors from an adjoining room. This could be the living room, nursery or study of a typical modern house, or a sun room in a corner of the garden. The glass doors opened on to a wide terrace spacious enough for entertaining and with a built-in brick barbecue. The terrace overlooked a broad sheet of water – perhaps a swimming pool or a dammed stream – beyond a retaining wall which gave additional casual seating for guests.

The suburban garden tends to have a definite division between the front, or public, part and the rear, or private, area. The front garden presents the visual impact on entering the house, but at the same time the designer is faced with the problem of the front approach being an access for cars. While the owner may be prepared to negotiate a tricky turning space, his family is less likely to, his visitors might try but tradesmen definitely will not. The result is crushed planting, broken kerbs and skid marks on the lawn. Thus an ample forecourt or a convenient junction for a U-turn is required; it is mean dimensions which wreak havoc with a garden. Ideally a turning space for the grand sweep round needs to be 40ft across.

Besides this, it may be that standing room is needed for a boat, horsebox or caravan, none of which improves the approach to a house. A separate building is, of course, ideal for parking any of these out of sight, but suburban properties seldom have such accommodation. It may be worth having a solid structure built as a continuation of a garage frontage and in the same material, even if only a single wall, to screen extra vehicles and possibly an oil storage tank. If there is no room to drive a car behind such a structure, and when the strip of land between the house/garage and site boundary has become the car park, a light timber frame might be erected over the top of the area, picking up the line of the upper edge of the ground-floor windows or the base of the garage roof. The framework can support climbers and, in fact, this additional parking space can be made to look as though it was intentional and not just an afterthought to the original plan.

Entrance to a property may be marred by a meanly proportioned footpath from the parked car to the front door, with such hazards as ill-lit unexpected steps; rock plants amid wobbling paving; and low hanging baskets. The owner is aware of their presence, but a stranger coming or going on a dark evening may see them – or not – in quite a different light.

The garden at the rear or side of the house is for family use. Its purpose is often that of an outside playroom. If there is sufficient space, you might allow for such features as a tree in which children can climb or swing or build a retreat. In a large-sized garden, this play area should be out of sight of the house, as children are not noted for their tidiness and adult supervision can ruin a glorious fantasy world. When the young members of the family grow up and leave home, the rear part of the garden may develop more towards horticultural display. But the owner should bear in mind that what is manageable at forty becomes a chore at sixty, so the design should be adaptable to changing circumstances.

In some areas, such as the wooded periphery of Paris and in London's home counties, the country in the shape of trees and rhododendrons creeps into the suburban garden, becoming a major asset around which to plan the rest of the layout. When starting from scratch, you should fight with your

Our suburban garden at the Chelsea Flower Show was intended to be only a part of a larger area. The structure on the terrace above the pool could be a house extension, a nursery or a sun room. The terrace was wide enough for play, entertaining or sunbathing, and incorporated a built-in barbecue on the left.

Storage space built into the boundary wall usefully near a sandpit to take the inevitable clutter of toys.

life to preserve existing trees from the builder's bulldozer. It is far easier for the builder to work on a cleared site than to take avoiding action the whole time, and the fact that a tree has a preservation order on it does not necessarily stop him from mauling it, for the penalty is small compared with the price he is getting for the house. Make sure that new levels do not rise round your trees or up their stems. Additional weight on their roots, a load of soil or dumped bricks will all harm if not kill. Fence off your trees to the line of their overhang, to protect them from damage by scaffolding, lorries and bonfires.

When evolving a layout for the suburban garden, first decide what you want to be able to do and where are the best places to do it – bearing in mind convenience of access, sun and shade, views to be blocked or emphasised, and any existing features. Note these down on the site plan and bind all the

A tree house, built in a conveniently shaped willow, provides endless hours of fun for children. The structure is both solid and safe, but still allows children using it to have some measure of fantasy in their play.

elements together in one overall pattern. This can be worked off the building module of your house or from a boundary line, or you can devise a system of your own. Broadly, one overall shape should encompass all, with incidents in it. A rose garden, herbaceous border or vegetable plot may be worked in by alternating areas of planting – preferably shrub and tree for ease of maintenance – with areas of paving. The whole is typically drawn together by a central grass area.

When you think you have evolved a reasonable layout, try to reverse it in your mind's eye, as you might look at the negative of a photograph. Both the positive and the negative aspects – that is, the bulky patches and the flat pieces in between, in whatever materials they are subsequently built – should appear proportionately attractive and well balanced.

The correct balance of a garden is not necessarily a symmetric tit for tat on either side of a central

Right: *circular concrete slabs, first as stepping stones and then as a feature within the pool in the suburban garden. The ground cover planting includes* Saxifraga umbrosa *(London Pride), hostas and lamium.*

The existing apple trees in this newish garden were maintained and they provide its chief feature. The foreground bench-seat surrounds the mulberry seen overhead. Note the visual strength of planting tulips of the same colour, later to be followed by marigolds.

Left: *the sun room of the suburban garden led straight out on to its terrace. The character of the whole garden was of simple modern lines contrasted with bright colours.*

Well-contrasted groups of plants fit into the overall scheme. If the basic pattern of the garden is strong enough – in this case one of gravel, brick walls and concrete paving – it will not be destroyed by plants which encroach onto and over it. The use of paved edging overcomes the problem of mowing up to creeping plants.

Left: *country garden furniture of brown basket-weave.*

path. It can equally well be an asymmetric arrangement, for few modern properties lend themselves to the pure symmetry of the formal gardens of le Nôtre in France.

Having worked out your rough plan, it must then be realised not only in shrubs, grass and so on but in building materials too. Architectural styles in the suburban situation vary according to the age of the house and its location, but the end result of the garden design should have its own identity – being neither too urban and sophisticated nor too rural. However, there are many suburban locations where stone would seem utterly out of scale and character, while elsewhere houses built of stone can justifiably be echoed in the garden.

When in doubt about what paving material to use, choose one so simple and straightforward that it cannot possibly offend. Concrete, sometimes much maligned, is ideal for such a situation. It is

A hard brick was used for both internal walling and some areas of paving. The circular islands in the pool were of cast concrete. Some of the boundary walling was in coloured precast concrete block.

A more extravagant form of concrete walling which looks particularly attractive if used as a frame for a large-leaved climber.

A sculptural arrangement of plant forms around a small pool. The large leaves at the rear are sumach (Rhus typhina) *with* Yucca flaccida, *the upright rosemary and hosta in the foreground.*

available in large slabs – square, rectangular, hexagonal and circular – or small tiles; there are also interlocking sections for drives.

An economic way to pave large areas is to use brushed concrete. It is laid *in situ* in squares no more than 12ft across either way, to avoid cracking, and preferably with reinforcement. The defining line to the squares can be brick, sett, concrete slab or even hardwood. The effect is of a large chequer-board and, if this is reduced in scale by halving or quartering the large squares and then infilling with paving or plants, the outcome can be an attractive terrace.

Our design called for brushed concrete to be laid through the brick stripes of the terrace. The sun room, retaining wall and much of the surfacing was of the same sand-faced honey-brown brick. On the rear wall of the site, white vinyl panels infilled a timber screen, reflecting the spacing and proportion of the sun-room windows.

Your walls can be built of solid concrete blocks or perforated screen blocks, or made of concrete cast *in situ*. If you cast your own concrete, do check on its reinforcement. The Cement and Concrete Association, 52 Grosvenor Gardens, London SW1, publishes splendid booklets to help you.

Once the pattern has been defined, the infilling of plant material can begin. The trees should be placed first, particularly those with a functional role in your layout. A tree of exaggerated form, such as a weeping willow or a fastigiate (upright) conifer, will need a special position in the basic plan. On our terrace, a key feature was a weeping willow contained in a built-in raised brick box.

When selecting plants, start with tall subjects for background screening and generally to hold and define the area, placing choicer, shorter ones in the foreground. Planting thus provides the bulk to the plan; all that is left is the space between. Since most suburban gardens are for the enjoyment of younger members of the family, and as father likes to see 'a bit of green' after his day at the office, the usual preference for the infill is a grassed lawn.

For a new area, you must decide between seeding and turfing. The difference in price is negligible in the long run, the initial outlay on turf being barely greater than for seed. There is also the question of labour necessary to prepare a seed bed, weed, de-stone and first cut a seeded area, along with the chore of watering when sowing has been done in dry weather. Turf, too, will need adequate watering. If well laid, it should start to root in a month or so and be usable after two months. A seeded lawn might take up to six months before it can be used; meanwhile fencing and constant vigilance will be needed to keep young children off it.

A lawn of thyme or camomile is not only costly to plant up, but takes very little wear. Certainly it could never stand a game of football being played on it – ideally your lawn shouldn't either, but tell that to the kids! The alternative to grass is more paving, which will be costly to construct and urban in appearance, while an area of gravel would probably prove unusable by a young family.

A pond can be a real asset to a suburban garden. Water is always a focal point and when used properly is very attractive. However, a thin stream splashing through plastic rocks only fusses and disturbs the layout. Water can be used in one of two ways: informally, where the surface outline is blurred with a beach or boggy planting, or in a more formal style, where the division between pool and surround is quite sharp, so that it appears as a sort of canal edged by grass or paving. If the area of water is large enough, these treatments can be used on either side.

In our suburban garden, the sheet of water beyond the terrace was perfectly still, so as to reflect the sky and overhanging willow branches. The water was contained in a black butyl rubber sheet, anchored by cobbled beaches on two sides and retained in the walling of the other sides. This type of sheeting

Stepping stones of various sizes act as islands through the low ground cover planting and continue as a feature into the pool, like huge water lilies. They are contrasted with masses of vertical-shaped water iris.

can be effective over a large area, but it is essential that any folds and all the edges of the material are carefully disguised. Broad areas of mixed planting ran into the cobble beaches to soften their outlines. Circular concrete discs were laid as stepping stones through the planting and continued as little islands into the pond. These were interplanted with water iris to create interesting vertical shapes in contrast to horizontal planes.

Before deciding on a natural pool for your garden, ask yourself if you want reflections in still dark water, or tranquil water lilies, or the sound of fountains playing, or the chatter of water over rocks. It is seldom possible to have more than one of these features in a suburban garden pond, as each has a strong individual character. So, pick the one most suitable for the site. The pool should be positioned where it might occur naturally, so the ground surrounding it blends with it as one unified conception.

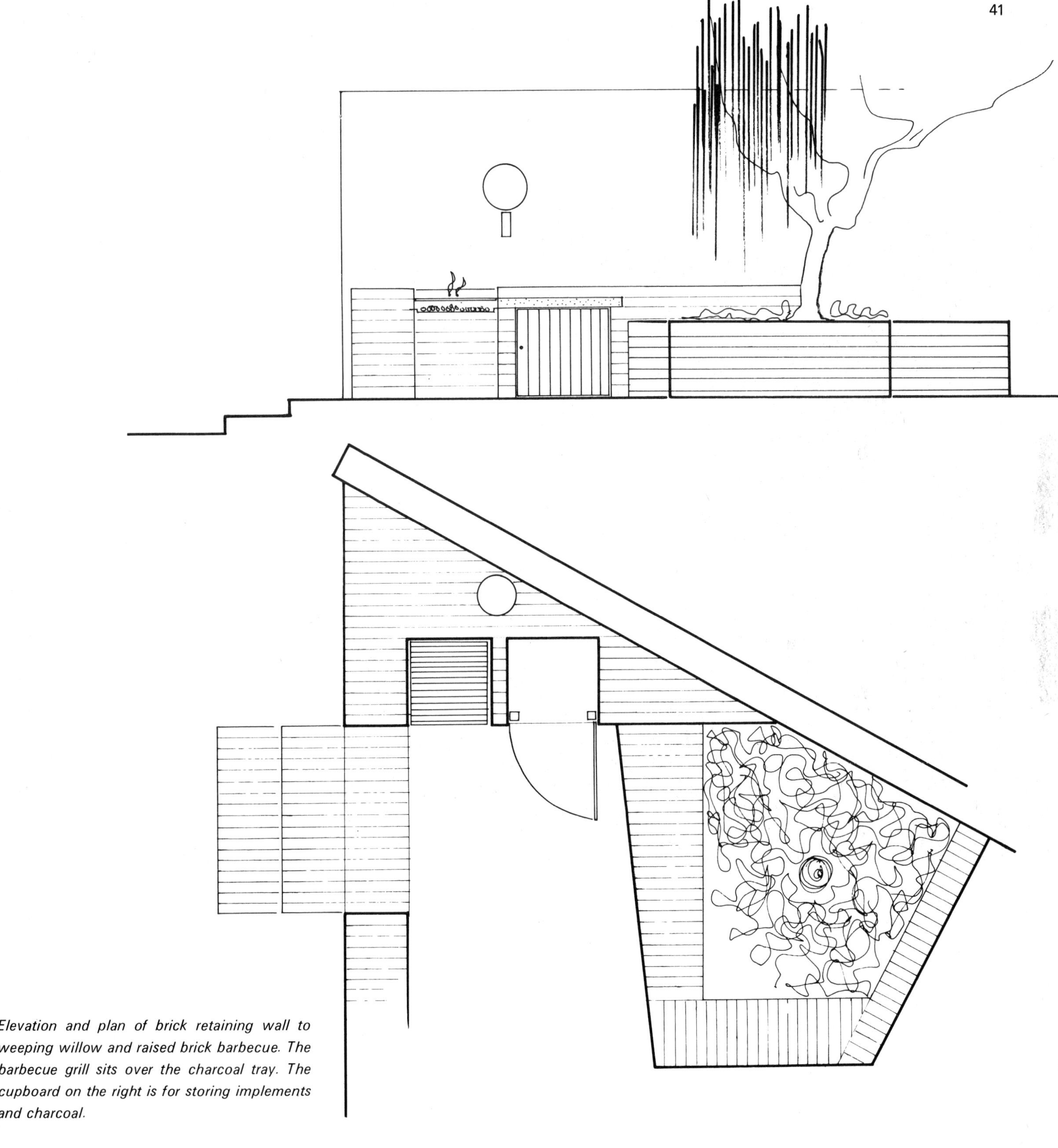

Elevation and plan of brick retaining wall to weeping willow and raised brick barbecue. The barbecue grill sits over the charcoal tray. The cupboard on the right is for storing implements and charcoal.

The feel of the suburban garden was essentially modern. Smooth simple shapes were contrasted with bold foliage form and bright colour. The whole conception was drawn together by a concrete sculpture of doves by Marie Gill.

Now that the setting of the garden is established, it can be furnished – with pots, seats, statuary or sculpture; these will be incidental to the layout and not dominate it. Too often an owner, aware that his garden is not right, overdecorates it by way of compensation, when the fault is far more fundamental.

Our whole layout was drawn together by a modern concrete sculpture of two doves by Marie Gill which counterbalanced the weeping willow. Plain white fibreglass pots for annuals were grouped on the terrace, which was equipped with modern outdoor furniture of white fibreglass and white painted wood. The type of incident you select should as far as possible be in character with the house and your own style of living. Urns and balustrades, for instance, suggest gracious country-house surroundings and can become pretentious in a more modest setting. Smart white metal furniture is essentially urban – and almost always uncomfortable. The suburban garden needs a gentler touch. It seems that in this type of situation it is customary for furniture to be left outside, only the cushions being removed at the end of the day. The pieces chosen should therefore look attractive when not in use, as well as being weatherproof.

The total effect of our suburban garden was modern, as was the plan. It was one of contrasting shapes, drawn together by the use of only one or two sympathetic materials throughout. The planting extended this principle to produce a controlled scheme primarily of yellows, with a good proportion of plant material using strong, architecturally shaped leaves, in splendid contrast to the simple modern line of the house.

THE COUNTRY GARDEN

Surely the best place to garden is in the country. Both the town and the suburban garden look into themselves, denying as far as possible their immediate surroundings, while the country garden, with its more relaxed atmosphere, is not only a pleasanter place to be but provides a natural setting for the house. There is also a greater permanence about the country site, which should be a controlled version of its rural surround and sit comfortably within it. While a suburban garden in its protective area can take on almost any form to suit its current owner, the country garden, once made, should be left to nature. It is a place for forest trees, not Japanese cherries.

In the country there is often greater space available to tempt the owner to overplant and fuss the site, thus giving himself untold work which he may only surmount with difficulty at the end of a long week-end's toil. A simple design approach is needed. Labour is scarce and even if available often lacks the skill and finesse of the old-time gardener. So shapes must allow for the easy circulation of motor mowers and do-it-yourself machinery.

The character of the garden should emerge naturally from its site and surround. It should be based on the local stone, or absence of it, and on the type of soil and vegetation prevailing. When designing your layout and planting, follow the site characteristics and the result, no matter how new, must fit; ultimately, of course, the maintenance will be easier too. An obvious example of a gardener at odds with his site is the constant effort to grow acid plants on an alkaline soil. Each location has its own flora, be content with that and the outcome will be far more satisfactory.

When evolving a new layout or revamping an existing one, the garden can usually be divided into three or four areas. The first, immediately surrounding the house, forms the transition between 'in' and 'out'; this can run into the second part which includes any outbuildings and often incorporates the

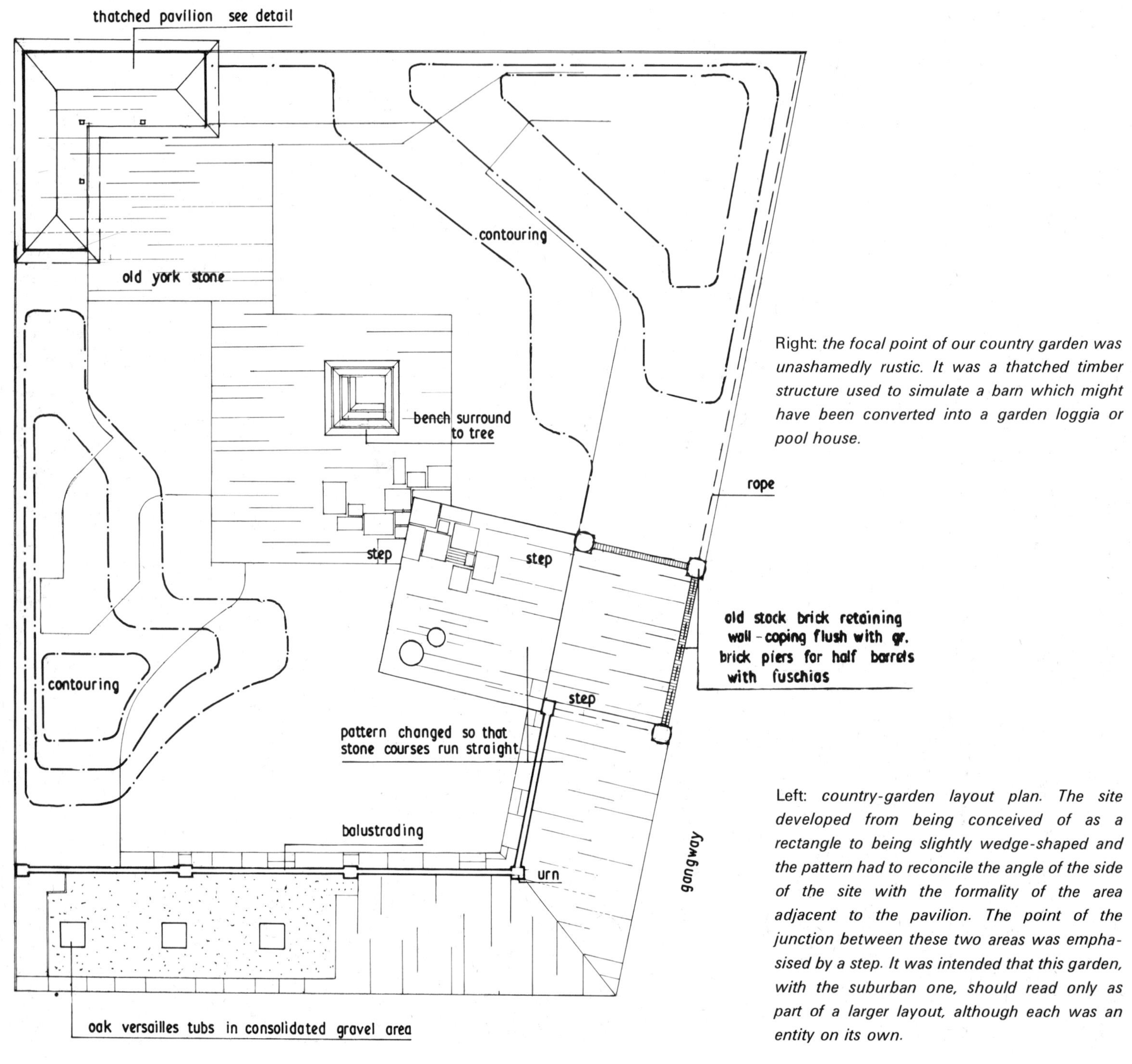

Right: *the focal point of our country garden was unashamedly rustic. It was a thatched timber structure used to simulate a barn which might have been converted into a garden loggia or pool house.*

Left: *country-garden layout plan. The site developed from being conceived of as a rectangle to being slightly wedge-shaped and the pattern had to reconcile the angle of the side of the site with the formality of the area adjacent to the pavilion. The point of the junction between these two areas was emphasised by a step. It was intended that this garden, with the suburban one, should read only as part of a larger layout, although each was an entity on its own.*

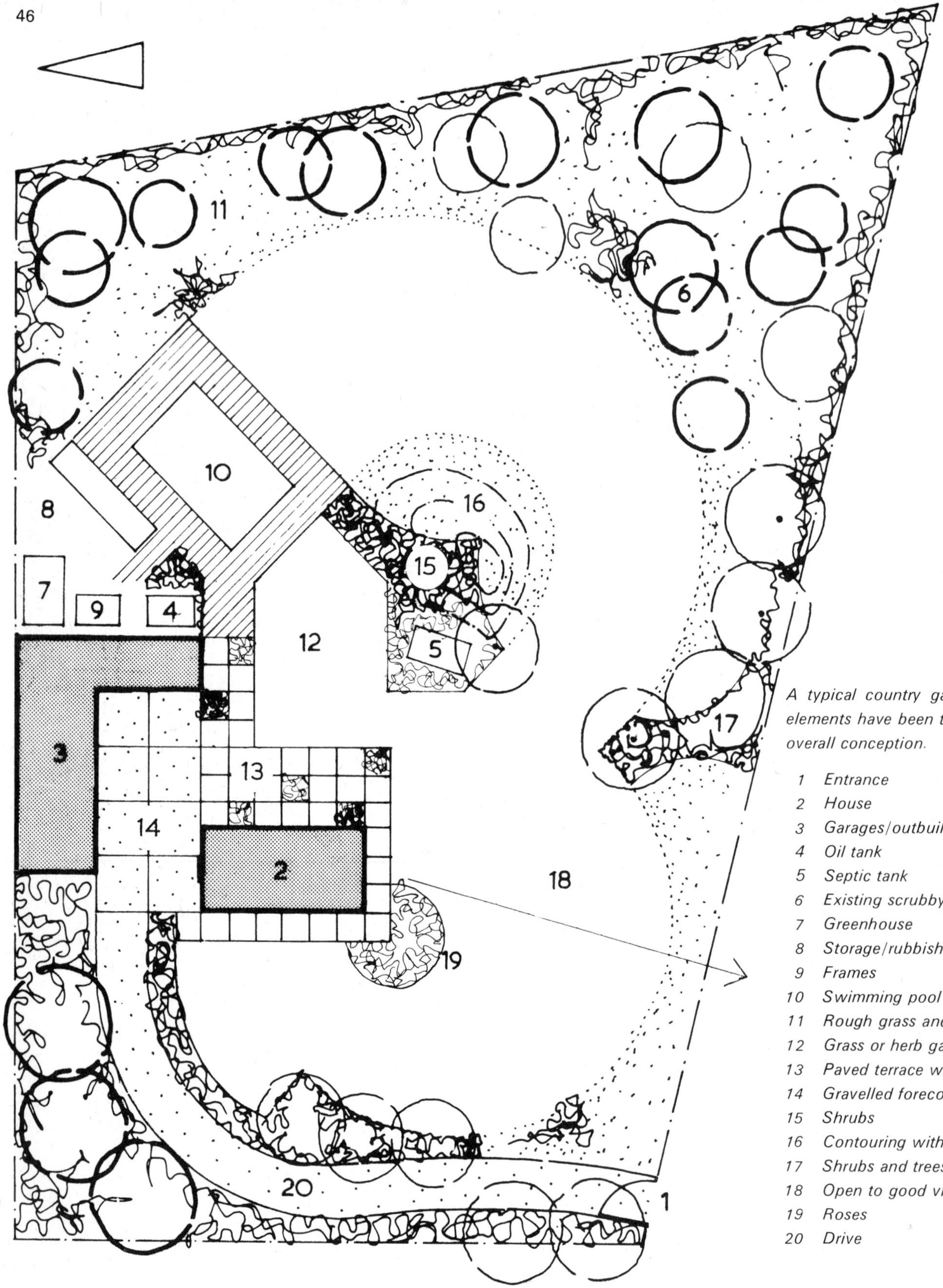

A typical country garden plan where various elements have been tied together in one strong overall conception.

1 *Entrance*
2 *House*
3 *Garages/outbuildings*
4 *Oil tank*
5 *Septic tank*
6 *Existing scrubby moorland*
7 *Greenhouse*
8 *Storage/rubbish area*
9 *Frames*
10 *Swimming pool and filtration changing*
11 *Rough grass and bulbs*
12 *Grass or herb garden area*
13 *Paved terrace with planting*
14 *Gravelled forecourt*
15 *Shrubs*
16 *Contouring with pool excavations*
17 *Shrubs and trees*
18 *Open to good view*
19 *Roses*
20 *Drive*

Ample brick-paved space has been allowed for eating out, play or entertaining in this country garden.

drive-in. What is left, the main part, can be designed very simply or sub-divided into sections for vegetables, roses, swimming, etc. Traditionally, as at Sissinghurst and Tintinhull, the garden was divided by hedges or screen plants into separate areas; the family just did not go into that part where nothing was happening. This approach seems barely possible now, since it involves large areas and considerable work. The modern version is to incorporate all the features into one sweeping design with only visual checks between.

The starting point in devising such a layout or adopting an older one is to list the family's requirements: a terrace, play area, service facilities, parking and wash-down spaces, fruit trees, etc. Then, on an accurate survey of the site, locate these according to convenience, access, sunlight, and unobstructed views. On the same grid method as for the town garden, evolve a design for the areas around the house, its entrance and any outbuildings. In this way the multiplicity of oddments are linked together. Bind all the other features running from this area in a meaningful sweep. The line should relate to the boundaries, to any views outside the site and to existing features within it. The sweep in reality becomes a contour line, a path, the edge of a mown area or a planted one.

In our country garden, wide steps led down from one end of the terrace to the shallow valley running diagonally across the site. The firm angled shape of the terrace and first landing locked into rectangular stone-and-brick paved areas which crossed the floor of the dell from an L-shaped arbour in the far corner. The arbour's open-fronted construction and thatched roof suggested a barn or outbuilding converted to garden use. A single tree – a stemmy rhododendron – in the centre of the dell was encircled by a timber bench seat, creating a pleasant place to sit and enjoy the garden, while the arbour could be used as an alternative on wet days, as well as being ideal for parties. These varied architectural features were intended to give the garden shape and coherence throughout the year.

Having outlined your layout on paper, check that it works on site by marking the pattern on the ground with canes or, on an existing lawn, with rope. Once the pattern is right, work at each component of the design in detail, deciding on your materials according to situation, character, availability and, of course, cost. Within the scale of a fair-sized country garden, one often has the opportunity to create interesting features – emphasising a good view or blocking a poor one – by ground shaping. This can be quite low – a 30° gradient from the horizontal is adequate – and still be effective, especially when used in conjunction with planting. In our country garden, the shallow valley was created by excavating ground from the central area to form contours on either side of the site. The apparent depth of the dell was emphasised not only by existing background trees but by large shrubs planted on top of the mounded slopes.

It is amazing what can be achieved in a single day with a bulldozer or similar earth-moving machine to entirely recreate levels and contours. A certain amount can be done on a cut-and-fill principle on a sloping site – ensuring that topsoil is removed and that basic shaping is achieved with subsoil before replacing the top; but much more is possible by the creation of gentle mounds. The result should look as though it had been there since time began. On no account should a bump appear like a burial mound – the amateur tends to make his contours too high and artificial.

By following as closely as possible the type of terrain surrounding the site, you will find you are working in natural curves. In nature a curve is never a mean thing or a wiggle; it is there for a reason – a stream meandering round an outcrop, a sheep track round a rock, a path round a tree – and it is this gentle curving line you seek to copy. Conversely, exciting results can be achieved – as at Dartington Hall, Devon – by chiselling the ground, in a way not unlike medieval man's lychets on a chalk down, although ultimate maintenance might prove a problem.

Another great opportunity for ground shaping is to use up excavated material from the construction of a swimming pool or other major building project, thus saving the cost of removing the soil to a dump. The earth can be placed to provide shelter or privacy for the pool, or to conceal it (it can look pretty depressing in winter). When planning such a swimming pool area, you may need to pinpoint the siting of a filtration plant, storage space for pool-cleaning gear and such refinements as changing and washing facilities, a bar, refrigerator, kettle point and perhaps even a telephone.

In the country, when considering surfaces, there is a tendency to muddle through – rusticity being the excuse. But, like well-laid, good quality carpet in the home, properly prepared paving is the basis of your garden. Unevenness causes standing water and cracking, and weeds will start to creep in. Such

The central area of the country garden was excavated out and the earth was used to build banks on either side of it. Old York stone terracing was then laid through the central area to the thatched barn. The garden was viewed on two sides from level paved terraces (which might surround the house), and which were retained by walling and balustrading by Chilstone.

Detail of urn and balustrade.

Left: *contoured mounds which framed the country garden were gentle and flowing and, above all, appeared as though part of nature. Care was taken so that they did not look like dumps superimposed on the ground.*

A punctuation mark in the old York stone paving which ran across the site to the barn was a fine double-stemmed rhododendron from Exbury. This was surrounded by a simple wooden bench seat.

a surface is not only irritating to use, but can be dangerous for elderly people and young children. In short, the area becomes something of a liability.

The materials used will very much depend on the extent of the areas to be paved. For a large surface, the more expensive old York stone may be out of the question, but cut stone, slate, brick, sett or grass when worked in can give very attractive results in sympathy with the surroundings. In our country garden design, old York stone was used with a brick infill for the paved areas. As an edging to a swimming pool, some of the textured slabs cannot be bettered for contact with bare feet.

Gardens have tended to develop in the parts left between paths, but this can be avoided if areas of paving – across which you can progress lineally – are worked into the overall pattern and a greater overall simplicity to the layout will result.

For a forecourt or drive, a washed river gravel (rounded) or chippings rolled into a hoggin layer over a base might be considered. By omitting patches of hoggin, the occasional shrub can be grown against a wall through the gravel finish. A tarmac surface has an unsympathetic hardness about it, though it will undoubtedly take heavy wear from cars or a horsebox. This could be given a coloured macadam finish or have gravel rolled into the final surface. White chippings spaced at intervals – so beloved by drive contractors – should be avoided; the result is brittle and urban. All hard surfaces should, of course, be drained with a cross-fall away from any building.

Other areas which are not paved, gravelled or planted will be laid to grass, or possibly derived from an existing pasture or sward. Changes of level are easy to cope with, as long as a reasonable gradient is allowed for mowing. Steeper slopes not needing to be traversed can be planted with a shrubby ground coverer, such as juniper, St John's wort (*Hypericum calycinum*) or a low-growing cotoneaster. The tricky part is in the construction of steps and retaining walls. It cannot be over-emphasised that some initial outlay to achieve a sound, long-lasting result is never wasted. It is worth spending money on broad, firm steps with properly constructed sides and good drainage.

Retaining walls, like steps, should be built on adequate foundations, with damp-proofing to preserve the wall and weep-holes at intervals along its base to forestall a build-up of water behind it. Make sure that the jointing is of a strong mix, and that the wall has a broad capping or coping. Resist any temptation to transform the wall into a rockery by leaving holes in it; these will weaken the structure and act as unwanted drainage outlets. It is better for plants to be grown on top of the wall so that they hang down. It makes economic sense to build walls of local material as far as possible. Flint or stone, for instance, tend not to be expensive and are often best suited to the style of the house. Avoid sham stone, which never seems to weather, and the regularity of its moulded irregularities does not deceive anyone into believing it is the genuine article. Concrete blocks are at least honest; they can be rendered or coloured, or coloured direct with a cement paint, but will need capping with a paving slab, tile or brick. Screen walling block, unless well clothed with plants, has a harshness about it that is better suited to the suburban situation.

Many rural areas have a fencing tradition and, rather than introduce an alien style, first explore the local possibilities. On the other hand, a ha-ha ditch to form the boundary line to the property will negate the necessity for fencing. Walling on a batter, at an angle, will probably be needed on one side of the ditch. The ha-ha should be deep enough to prevent cattle or horses crossing it, although fencing or an electric wire – placed inconspicuously along the base of the ditch – will deter them to a certain extent.

Over and above the economics of using local materials, the owner of a country property has a certain obligation to the area where he has chosen to live, and his house and garden should fit happily into these surroundings. When mature, the planting will be visible from quite a distance and the larger the garden the more important such considerations are, if the countryside is not to become suburbanised. This interaction between garden and rural landscape is vital. Presumably too the point of living in the country is to see something of it – if only at weekends. Too often the garden is enclosed as it would be in a town, whereas some opening up or the construction of a ha-ha might bring the surrounding countryside visually within its boundaries. By doing this, you can cut down on any rival attractions inside the garden and at the same time eliminate the need to look after them.

There is a limit to the sort of view which the viewer can take in. A panoramic sweep is seldom satisfying; it is better to aim for a limited outlook, framed by foreground planting – like a picture, in fact.

Planting for a damp site – note the great contrast in leaf shape and the gradations of green.

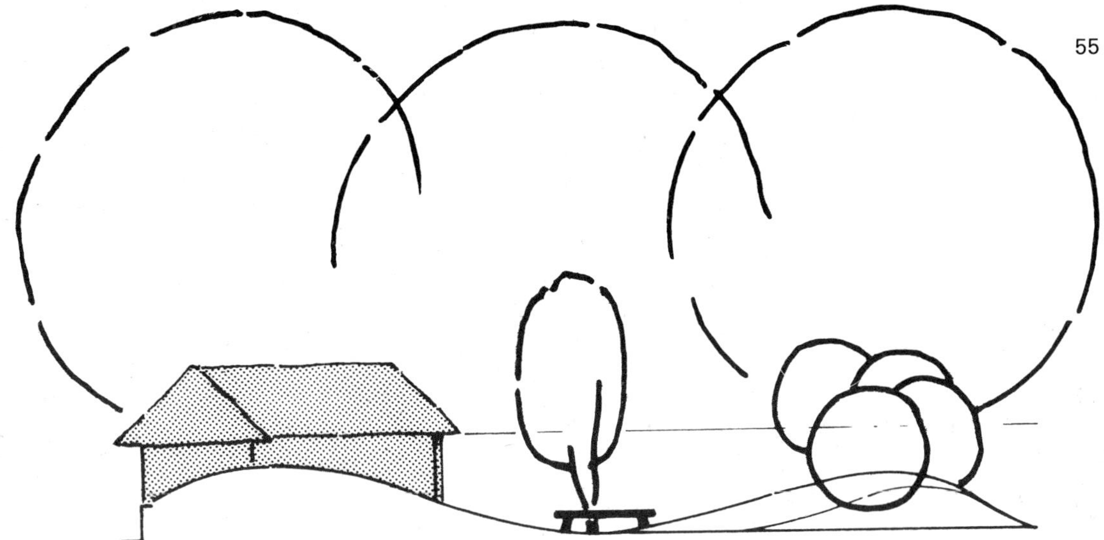

The basic ground-shaping of the country garden with earth excavated out and pushed to both sides. The paved terracing becomes more than just a path, with one half angled to the barn and the other, where there is a step, angled to the splay of the site boundary.

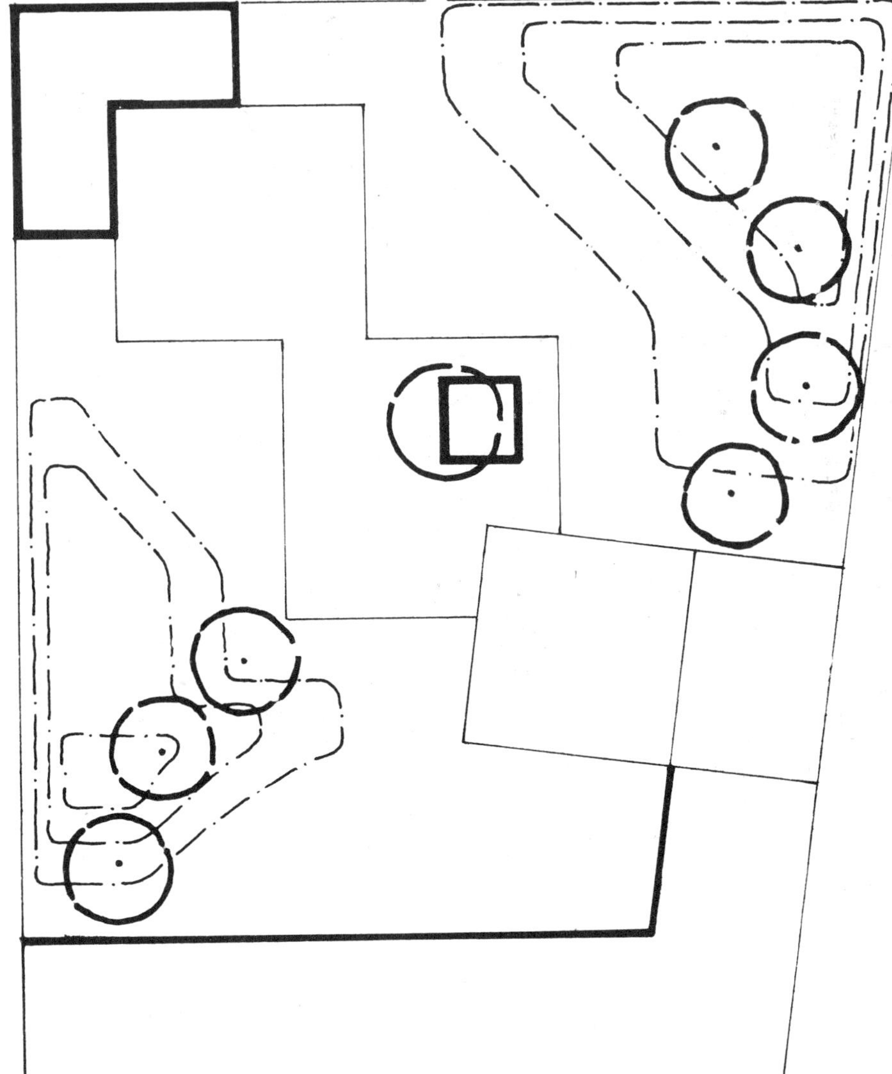

Opposite
Top: *the mixed herbaceous border.*
Bottom: *the flat heads of yellow achillea contrast well with the strap-like leaves of the day lily (hemerocallis) while tobacco plants (nicotiania) and grey* Stachys lanata *complete the group.*

A gentle sweep of mown grass linking two areas of a country garden. The bank should obviously be at a mowable gradient, but more important the top and bottom of the banks should be broadly rounded so that the mower neither scalps the brow nor misses the grass in the trough at the bottom of the bank.

Right: *where space allows, swimming pools can be screened behind sheltering walls which both cut down draught and provide a measure of privacy when in use and, moreover, hide the pool which in a temperate climate is not a stimulating sight to many for a considerable number of months in the year.*

A large country place will allow the owner to indulge himself with a swimming pool, tennis court and adequate supply of home-grown fruit and vegetables. These are all splendid in their way, but do not need to be visible at all times of the year. Vegetables, when not grown to excess, can look quite attractive, but rows of rotting Brussels sprouts are not a pretty sight.

Ideally, the vegetable garden should be as near the kitchen as possible and linked to it by a hard-surfaced access. In practice the vegetables often end up in a patch at the far end of the site. Planting divisions, contouring or even hedging can be used effectively to screen such an area. Avoid the rose-covered rustic trellis which does not do its job well all the year round.

Herbs need not be banished to a corner of the vegetable patch or kitchen garden. They can be grown decoratively in pots on the terrace, since many are evergreen, or mixed in among herbaceous and shrub planting, though most like an open, sunny situation.

When it comes to the siting of a greenhouse and frames, and tool and machine storage sheds, an otherwise visually peaceful garden can be wrecked by such disproportionately obtrusive structures. Try to mass them in a group, perhaps using one building to house them all. The lean-to shed-cum-greenhouse is another way of minimising their presence, while any existing outbuildings can be adapted for the storage of garden tools and mechanical aids.

Part 2

Planting

by Robin Lane Fox

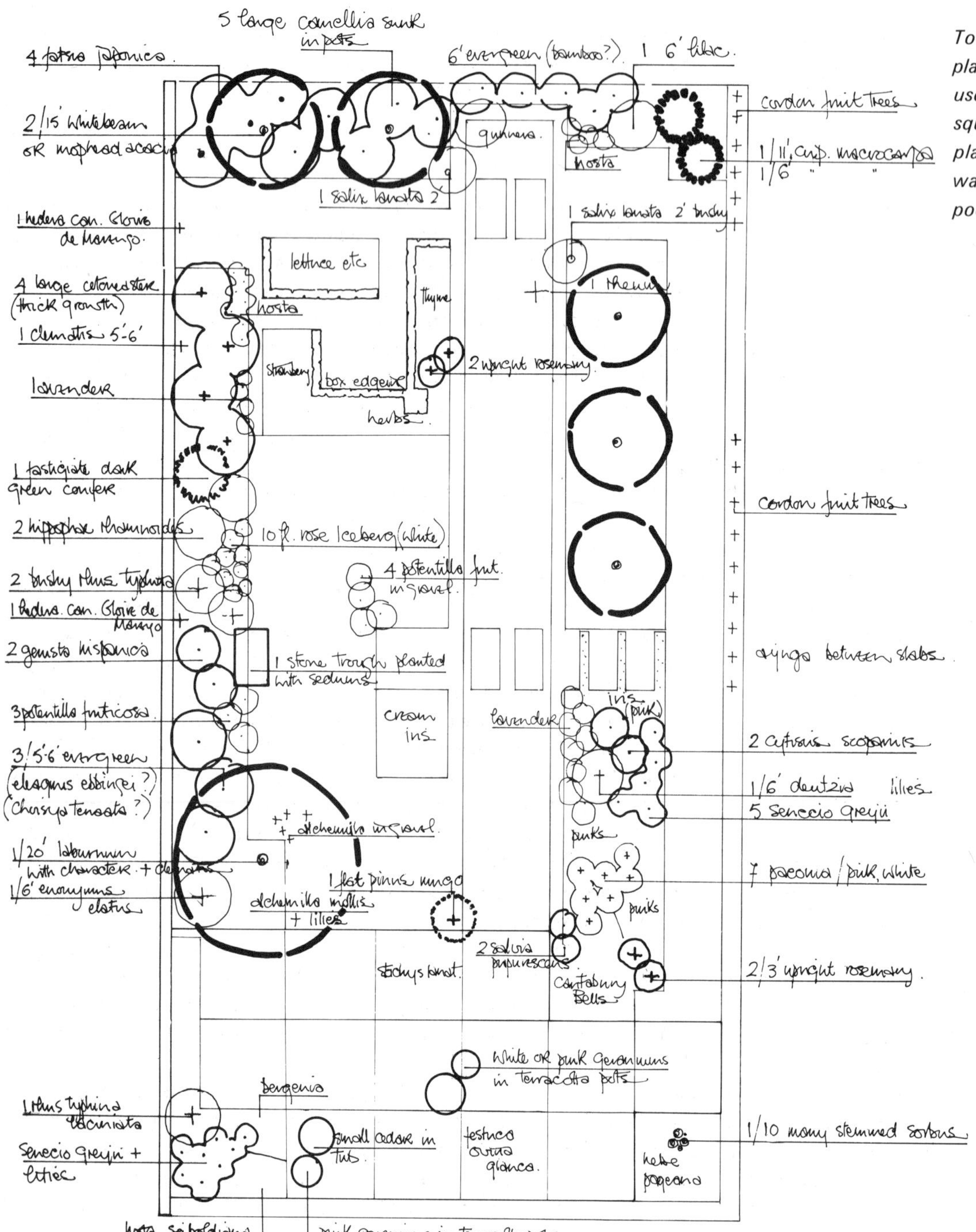

Town-garden planting plan. Foreground terrace planting with bold slabs of ground cover was used to contrast with the brick and paved squares. Beyond this, the long thin bed was planted with country subjects and this block was counterbalanced on the other side of the pool by a small herb and vegetable garden.

Fatsia japonica
2 15ft whitebeam or mop head acacia
Hedera canariensis *'Gloire de Marengo'*
4 large cotoneaster
5–6ft clematis
lavender
fastigiate dark green conifer
2 Hippophae rhamnoides
2 bushy Rhus typhina
2 Genista hispanica
3 Potentilla fruticosa
3 5–6ft evergreen (Elaeagnus ebbingei *or* Choisya ternata)
20ft laburnum with character, plus clematis
6ft Euonymus elatus
Rhus typhina *'Laciniata'*
Senecio greyii *plus lilies*
Hosta sieboldiana
bergenia
small cedar in tub
pink geraniums in terracotta pot
Festuca ovina glauca
white or pink geraniums in pots
Hebe pageana
10ft many-stemmed sorbus
Stachys lanata
Alchemilla mollis *plus lilies*
Alchemilla *in gravel*
stone trough planted with sedums
4 Potentilla fruticosa *in gravel*
10 floribunda roses 'Iceberg'
strawberry
herbs
2 upright rosemary
thyme
box edging
lettuce, etc
Salix lanata
5 large camellias sunk in pots
6ft evergreen (bamboo)
gunnera
hosta
6ft lilac
cordon fruit trees
11ft Cupressus macrocarpa
6ft Cupressus macrocarpa
2ft bushy Salix lanata
rheum
cordon fruit trees
Ajuga reptans *between slabs*
2 Cytisus scoparius
6ft deutzia
5 Senecio greyii
7 paeonia pink, white
2 3ft upright rosemary
canterbury bells
2 Salvia purpurascens
pinks
iris pink

It might be of interest to clarify how a design for a flower show garden evolves and to see why some of the planting details are so sketchy.

An initial scheme was prepared by John Brookes and submitted to the committee, who discussed it in detail. It was then priced for building by a landscape contractor. Lastly an outline of planting detail was produced which, after committee approval, was given to the contractor to put in hand.

The planting detail is only an outline, since often the plants first thought of are not readily available in the size and shape required. Nearly all the shrub material had to be larger than normal sales stock and so various nurseries were scoured for the right shrubs while other shrubs employed on previous occasions were also used. Herbacious and annual material had to be specially brought on and a lot of the material was supplied by specialist growers (many of whom were also producing material for their own stands and, not unnaturally, wanted the best plants for themselves).

For any show or exhibition the plants are not received from the various sources until actual planting time and then much always has to be rejected if it is not near its prime, so that the blooms are just opening as the judges go round. It is important to remember that to win a gold medal the garden has to be exemplary in every respect, not only in its design, so that the quality of individual plants is important as well.

Changes are always inevitable in the planting detail until the last minute, so that the final garden often bears no detailed resemblance to the original conception, although scale and colour ranges will have been adhered to.

'The size of a garden has very little to do with its merit. It is merely an accident relating to the circumstances of its owner. It is the size of his heart and brain and goodwill that will make his garden delightful or dull.' So wrote Miss Jekyll, perhaps our greatest planter of gardens.

THE TOWN GARDEN

With those comments in mind, we wanted a varied range of plants in our town garden which did not stress one kind of gardening too heavily, but we did not wish to plant a confused garden where too many plants would be shown in ones or twos without any recurring mass. A well-designed garden is not a collection. Often more kinds of plant accumulate than the eye can match together. We are always comforted by a clear style and by repetition, so our first principle was to mark clearly which plants could be included and to repeat the same background masses in order to link the planting plan together. We soon learnt that good planting is as much a matter of omitting plants as of putting them in.

Before you plant a garden, it helps to think of it as a face. It must have fine bones; it must have the smooth texture of a soft skin; its colouring must be subtle and not too strong; it must also be beautifully made up. It must reflect a mood and convey a sense of personality when its features are attractively combined. Bones, texture, colouring, decoration and, above all, mood are the features for which a garden must be planted.

As in our town garden, the bones are partly the line of the plan and partly the solid mass of background planting and permanent screens. In a large garden the trees too would hold the plan together, but in a smaller plot they are more of a decoration. Our main bones, therefore, were the more solid shrubs, bamboos and camellias, the thick mass of rhododendrons and the few screening plants which we could move when already well grown. The town gardener would indeed do well to use bamboos and camellias as the bones for his garden. Both are happy in town conditions which are usually shaded and often damp. They do not mind if they are planted in soil which is only as good as its recent enrichment with humus and manure or its leavening with peat – not itself a rich food of any importance.

Bamboo, especially, is a screen which will block out a fence, a neighbour, the end of a garden or the sides of a shed. It grows very fast, is easily increased by division with a sharp spade and can reach a height of 12ft. It has a mood of its own, as Japanese gardeners have long recognised, and we thought it suited our long canal of water, hiding its far end in an appropriate curtain of stems and green leaves. The easiest and most obliging varieties are *Sinarundinaria murielae*, up to 12ft tall with the usual narrow leaves, and *S. nitida*, slightly less vigorous but with the attraction of purple-green stems.

Camellias are glossy, flower-laden and less thick in their growth. Every gardener has his favourite; mine is still the *williamsii* hybrid 'Donation', raised at Borde Hill in Sussex, its semi-double, pink flowers veined with a darker pink drop when they turn brown and fade. This habit is not shared by many other camellias. Among whites, the ordinary 'Alba Simplex' resists the weather well; the hybrid 'Cornish Snow' resists it less well, but both are lovely. Remember that camellias do not like lime, hence they must have peat and be watered with rain-water if you live in a garden which cannot grow rhododendrons. To keep the peat free of the natural limey soil it can be laid in a hole 4ft deep lined with polythene sheeting. Spring frost often damages a camellia's buds, but a cage of nylon netting fixed over the plants in March will serve as a string vest to give the insulation of pockets of air which can keep off those final degrees of cold. Bamboos and camellias are both evergreens, an important point in any planting.

Left: *strong, straight lines, a solid mass of background planting and permanent screens form the bones of the small town garden.*

The camellia hybrid 'Donation' with semi-double pink flowers grows well in town or country.

The best bones in a garden persist throughout the year and at least two-thirds of them should be evergreen shrubs. Rhododendrons have many admirers, though their leaves are mostly dull. Others may prefer *Osmarea burkwoodii* with its scented white flowers in April. This magnificent shrub can either be clipped to shape or left to grow 18in a year. No garden is too humble for a clipped buttress of yew or, with patience, a mass of box. There is always room for the magnificent *Fatsia japonica* whose fingered leaves resemble those of an evergreen fig-bush. The variegated form is not so impressive, though it too thrives in shade or towns. *Ceanothus* flourishes in those corners of town gardens which are so often warmer in winter than a wall or cranny in the country. In a sunny place the finest evergreen species are *C. burkwoodii* and *C. dentatus*, though neither is infallibly hardy.

All these evergreens will do well in a town garden and reach a screening height of at least 6ft, though yew is sometimes reluctant to grow freely away from clean air. Avoid holly because its prickly leaves are a menace to anyone who is weeding an enclosed small space. Other screeners, less bold in shape and mass, but willing to grow fast in shade and poor soil, are the semi-evergreen cotoneasters, especially *Cornubia* with huge bunches of red autumn berries and *C. rothschildianus* with yellow berries. Both are rapid and easy, though their outline is rather awkward. The yellow-flowered, quick-growing *Berberis stenophylla* is thick with very prickly stems and rapidly makes a flowering hedge which can be pruned lightly twice a year. It is worth cutting it back hard in its first two years to stop it becoming thin at the bottom. Avoid the tall evergreen *Viburnum rhytidophyllum* unless the dank leathery leaves, borne uncomfortably on its branches, are more to your taste than to mine. Winter-flowering laurustinus – another evergreen viburnum (*V. tinus*) – forms a far prettier backbone for the garden, though it is not particularly fast growing. Almost all hedging conifers, especially the quick-growing kinds, are hideous to my eye, so please be critical before you plant them. Very few stop at a modest height or shape. One of the fastest is *Cupressocyparis leylandii*, but its shaggy grey-green screen is dull and soon becomes too loose.

A terrace, such as the one in our garden, should also be classed as a permanent bone, not least because its bold pattern of blue brick and plain paving-slabs is constant throughout the year. The large blocks of low planting should be varied and kept in clearly defined beds to match the shape of their paving. Plants scattered informally between paving-stones make walking difficult and chairs too will catch on them.

Melissa officinalis aurea, *the golden-leaved lemon balm.*

In our garden the front of the terrace was massed with the golden-leaved lemon balm, listed as *Melissa officinalis aurea*. Its scented leaves grow neatly in spring, but in high summer it becomes taller and less tidy, and can then be cut to the ground to sprout for the autumn season. A gardener would prefer the tidy grey-leaved *Hebe* 'Pagei', another evergreen bone which we massed for its spreading stems, its long-lasting white flowers and low habit – some 9in high. The silver variegated thyme 'Silver Queen'; the herb hyssop, with pink and mauve-violet flowers, a free-flowering relation of the catmint, called *Calamintha nepetoides*; a sun rose with ash-grey leaves, such as *Helianthemum* 'Wisley Primrose'; lavender in its dark Hidcote form or the unusual *Lavandula stoechas* for warmer gardens; a central clump of the hardy *Agapanthus* Headbourne Hybrids, whose violet-blue flower-heads are my favourite sight in an August border – this selection, mostly in leaf throughout the year, could fill a terrace without looking mean or dull. There might even be room in a corner panel for some 3ft high bushes of *Daphne odora*, an easy shrub to grow and increase from cuttings in any sunny bed. Its mauve-white flowers are borne in spring and are more sweetly scented than those of any other shrub which has yet come to my notice. It can also be enjoyed in a 7in pot as a terrace plant and taken indoors to avoid the damaging frost in winter.

To the right of our small canal we set apple trees in the surface of the gravel and continued the idea down the right side of the garden where we planted espalier-trained apple trees instead of a hedge. No garden is too small to include fruit trees, whose blossom and fruit give two seasons of interest. It was one of our principles to break the divisions between fruit, flower and vegetable beds. Gardeners who are willing to sacrifice some of their fruit crop for a third season of flower should try planting a moderately vigorous climber among their fruit trees. They might choose a wild form of clematis, such as a *viticella* or *montana* variety, or a manageable rose, such as 'Paul's Lemon Pillar' or even a Dutch honeysuckle. These are placed at the foot of a fruit tree and can hoist themselves into the branches on a cage of wire-netting wrapped round the trunk. The strong rose 'Bobbie James', with its clusters of scented

Breaking the division between fruit and flowers, Clematis montana *is here shown in association with* Morus *nigra.*

white button-flowers, gives new life to a pear tree in early July. The very vigorous *Rosa filipes* 'Kiftsgate' and other rampant ramblers are only suitable for tall, strong trees, as they will smother and kill most fruit-trees with their thick growth, but a modest climber will make the most of a small tree without taking up more ground. Such experiments can extend the space of the smallest garden.

The disadvantage of fruit trees is that they look bare and spindly in winter. It might be preferable to have several small trees which are more attractive during this season when a garden's bones are so prominent. The most startling, though the most expensive, is *Acer griseum*, a form of maple which grows slowly to 15ft. It leaves its old bark to peel off in thin torn strips, which are yellowish red during the winter, and reveal a clean and polished red-brown trunk underneath. The winter cherry, *Prunus subhirtella autumnalis*, is more conventional, bearing clouds of frail white blossom from November

The old bark of Acer griseum *peeling off to reveal the red-brown, polished trunk underneath.*

onwards. Though a sharp frost will brown its buds, their season is a long one and the tree's shape is always pretty. Old winter cherries can grow surprisingly large, even if birds sometimes strip their flowers. A background of dark evergreen leaves, such as those on our bay trees, sets off its white winter flowers very clearly. This accompaniment also suits the winter-flowering viburnums, especially the admirable form called *V. bodnantense* 'Dawn'. This tall shrub reaches a height of 10ft; it bears its clusters of pink-white flowers on the tips of its bare branches from autumn to spring. It is sweetly scented, like many winter shrubs, and the young flowers have a peppery flavour to them which makes one sneeze. It could be combined with an ornamental crab-apple tree (*Malus*), either the red-fruited 'John Downie' or the yellow-fruited 'Golden Hornet'. Their heavy crops of bright fruit are as gay as any flower in the winter months and are not particularly attractive to birds. They grow some 20ft high

Taxus baccata, *a strong focal point in any garden.*

eventually and can be classed as a suitable bone for small gardens because of their firm shape and lasting season of interest. All these winter trees and shrubs would stand happily and neatly in a surfacing of gravel.

Our trees needed a background and we decided on a pointed tree or shrub of fastigiate or pyramidal shape. Preferring an evergreen, we grouped some tall bay trees, a pretty choice for a garden which is not too frosty in winter. I have grown bays on the edge of the Cotswolds, but I would not risk them farther north unless I could rely on the special protection of the Gulf Stream or a very well-sited wall. Many gardeners would turn to a pyramid conifer instead, a chamaecyparis or a cupressus. Their dank feathery outline is not a pleasing one and in most landscapes or small gardens they look out of place. Their leaves are often smelly; this would be a disadvantage near a seat, a feature which we placed among our pyramid bays. The pointed conifer shape could be enjoyed more naturally by planting a fastigiate yew in a dark green form; the golden form is brash and unnecessary as the spring growth on a yew is yellow-green anyway. A fastigiate hornbeam is another tree of an attractively pointed shape, though it is not evergreen. Whitebeams, beech, oak, Norway maple and birch are only a few of the forest trees which have smaller fastigiate forms, so useful to the discerning gardener. A pointed tree is an important bone as it breaks up a background and suggests a firm stop to a planting. This full stop was needed at our garden's far end. Shrewd planting depends on a knowledge of the wide and unfamiliar range of shapes available in garden plants. A rose bush, for instance, can arch, stand upright, droop, splay sideways or run as a prickly thicket.

The bones of our garden did not lie only round its corners and extremities. Opposite our fruit trees we planted a formal pattern of clipped box hedging to mark out the lines for a small bed of vegetables. This attracted more attention than any other features and must be considered carefully. There are differing schools of thought about this traditional box hedging. Those who dislike box complain, often correctly, that it gives cover to snails and slugs, becomes infested with bindweed, needs to be clipped annually, and dies back in the middle, especially when dogs cock their legs on it. But slug-baits are effective nowadays; bindweed will not suddenly intrude if the ground has been well cleaned and poisoned before planting, while any edging, especially grass, needs clipping and weeding. Box is an admirable bone for a garden which is keenly maintained. It is neat, evergreen, and can frame any garden picture in a formal circle. It can be arranged to give a monogram of its owner's initials, a badge, crest, emblem or straight line of green leaves. The finest form is a small variety which is variegated with silver along the edge of its leaf and named after E. A. Bowles. It is very slow growing, but so is the more usual *suffruticosa*, the neatest green variety for a hedge. Box should be planted deeply and, in my opinion, is better when not fed or manured. It prefers lime.

From box, the smallest evergreen bone, we moved on to plants – the skin and features of our garden. We chose these for their leaves as much as for their flowers, placing them in drifts between the bones and the short-lived cosmetics of bright colour. For instance, our box-edged bed was filled with strawberries and small vegetables, a planting which is too often separated from the flower garden's view. This filling was itself a feature, for there is beauty as well as taste in many edible plants. The leaves of strawberries have an elegant outline and will edge a bed as thickly as many of the more usual carpeting plants. The new variety 'Grandee' bears its bright fruit for a long season and should replace the older and more troublesome forms.

Yet the finest-tasting strawberry is a wild one – the alpine 'Baron Solemacher'. It is particularly generous but not easily increased as it does not throw out runners. Unless you are rich, the need for a

A formal pattern of clipped box hedging marks out the lines for a small vegetable bed of pretty and useful lettuce, carrots, tomatoes and chives.

large number will force you to the easy pleasure of growing it from a seed-packet. Alpine strawberries are a valuable feature for the skin of any small garden in town or country. They can be raised cheaply from seed sown in September and will fruit the following summer. They must be fed frequently and never left short of water. If watered heavily, they do not resent the shade. Remember to mass your plants. The fruits are borne above the ground and despised by birds because they are small.

An amusing companion would be the ornamental or 'flower' forms of cabbage and kale. These are best raised from seed and planted out for their season of beauty lasting from the cooler days of autumn well into winter. Their curled, frilled and variegated leaves are unlike those of any other feature. Some of these cabbages are flushed with white, some blush with pink and purple; others are twisted and

Top: *the decorative form of the globe artichoke 'Gros Vert de Laon'.*
Above: *chives* (Allium schoenoprasum) *in flower.*

crimped like a popular style of Victorian china. They seem to have been carved or cut into shapes which no other foliage plant can equal. They are slow during the summer to reach maturity, but in late August and September I could examine and admire them for a longer time than any other intricate leaf, especially after an autumn dew or an early frost. They are not recommended for eating and have an unpleasant smell when their leaves fade.

Fruiting vegetables can be enjoyed by planting red and yellow capsicum peppers, sweet corn and, of course, tomatoes, which are more decorative and no less edible in their yellow-fruited forms. Large gardens or bold borders could find room for the noblest vegetable of all: the globe artichoke, whose large grey leaves arch outwards from a neat clump until growth begins in May. After that, 5ft high stems spoil the clump's neatness, but they are soon forgiven when they bear those edible buds which look so elegant and taste so delicious. Pick them before they open into their lavender-blue heads of flower; boil them and put them under a poached egg. Be sure to buy a named variety, such as 'Gros Vert de Laon'. Artichokes are easily raised from seed, but few seedlings have fat and succulent buds and are thus a waste of the gourmet's time. Artichokes are not long lived but can be divided with a sharp spade. Straw protects them from the frost they hate and which kills them in cold winters. They like a well drained soil and settle more quickly if sand or gravel is mixed heavily with it.

Vegetables should also be considered for their flowers and for their value as a screen. Broad beans, chives and even the unusual varieties of mange-tout peas would be valued by flower gardeners were they not so dogmatically confined to the allotment or kitchen-patch. Broad beans, especially, with their black and white flowers and silky grey-green leaves could merit a place in the most exclusive border. When we pick beans, we are only dead-heading – a task which many border plants require of us. Runner beans make a quick and pleasant screen if trained on ornamental posts. This job is sometimes given to the quick-growing annual hops. Shrewd gardeners know the value of golden or variegated hops for the first year in a garden of bare walls. Such a screening of beans or hops can intrude into the central space of a garden and divide it into alluring bays and recesses. At a lower level, a solid edging of the crimped leaves of green parsley will almost serve by itself as a bone to a corner of any plan. There are few prettier leaves (the Greeks gave them away in garlands to victorious athletes) and just because we eat them we should not forget to enjoy looking at them.

Away from vegetables, there are the more usual drifts of leaves which make up the features of modern gardens. Hostas, bergenias and *Senecio laxifolius*, that splendid grey-leaved shrub, are the holy trinity of modern garden design. The first two grow in any town or shade; the third also thrives in a city and is almost immune to frost and winter damp. The flowers of all three are unimportant, but a garden's features last longer if they depend on a plant's leaves, not on a mere fortnight's blossom. A bergenia's leaves are bold; the hostas' are many-coloured, never more so than in the admirable *H. fortunei albo-picta* whose young growth is suffused with lime yellow in May. I also recommend the more unusual *H. undulata univittata* whose narrow, modest leaves are marked with a central band of white. Hostas prefer shade, rich soil, manure and a place away from slugs which ruin their leaves. Their pale mauve flowers appear more freely in sun, but their leaves are then less lush. They die down in autumn, turning a gay shade of yellow first. They grow anywhere, provided you do not spike their buds with a fork when they are dormant in winter. Together with the 3ft-high mounds of senecio there are no more reliable features with which to match a garden's bones. The senecio will grow 4ft wide in summer and bear flowers like a yellow ragwort unless you pinch out the tips of its stems in spring. This pinching keeps it compact and stops it from bearing its harsh flowers. We should all pinch back our

Right: *a scree garden – possibly a better way to grow alpines where there is no natural rock available for a rockery.*

Hosta undulata univittata.

small shrubs and taller border plants more regularly in late spring. It saves the business of staking them in summer and it can cause them to grow into more original shapes.

I see the value of the bergenia, for there are so few small evergreen plants with a firm bold leaf, but I usually dislike it. A modern hybrid called 'Silberlicht' does have tolerable grey-white flowers, but the common rose-pink flower heads of ordinary forms do not appeal to me. The leaves though not thrilling are dependable. Dead bergenias are a rarer sight than dead donkeys. If you use them, I hope you will mass them and only buy the very best leaf, to be found in the expensive kind called 'Ballawley Hybrid'. This does at least turn a prettier shade of red in autumn than the bilious flush on the leaves of other glossy bergenias. I would confine them to the most difficult corners or the darkest recesses, if only there were more obvious alternatives to replace them in more favoured positions.

Left: *a mixed border of iris, anchusa and oriental poppies.*

Bergenia ciliata, *cultivated as much for its attractive foliage as its flowers.*

Left: *soft greys, pink and blue, complement the old grey stone of this garden.*

Bold evergreens for the front of a border are not easily found. I would plead for more use of the variegated forms of certain irises, especially *Iris foetidissima* whose leaves, when broken, smell of roast beef. If only the small rosettes of London Pride and its vast crop of airy pale pink flower were bigger, they would put those of a bergenia to shame. So, too, would the glossier leaf of *Waldsteinia ternata*, like an evergreen strawberry, or the cream variegations of the small bugle (*Ajuga reptans variegata*).

Having outlined the bones and features of the garden, we are ready for the decoration. Sweet williams, canterbury bells, forget-me-nots and even wallflowers are invaluable for a town gardener who can afford to buy fully grown plants in late spring or who has space to raise his own, being sure to sow their seeds in the May of the year before they will flower. Wallflowers can also be kept going by

The useful Iris foetidissima *has attractive fruits and strange-scented leaves.*

The orange daisies of Ursinia anethoides.

Paving broken up by a water-feature containing cobbles, in the Japanese style.

cuttings taken in late spring and grown on for the following season. Once the biennials have flowered they can be rooted out, leaving space for the summer bedding, which anyway is better when not planted out too early. This pleasing and brief labour gives you two long seasons, not requiring too much of an effort in a small space.

Only one worthwhile biennial will give you a long show by itself and last throughout the summer. This is the neglected Brompton stock, which can be sown in August, wintered either in a sheltered bed or in a frame, then planted out in April for its six-month season of flower in summer and autumn. Its white or rosy mauve flowers are not the most pleasing colours, but dead-head it and enjoy its scent. It is better if kept for only one flowering season. It combines well with white snapdragons, petunias and the neglected dimorphotheca. I would also wish to include the Marvel of Peru, *Mirabilis jalapa*, a perennial for the adventurous; the wonderfully blue yet uncommon phacelia; sweet woodruff; the blue pimpernel or anagallis; fussy gazanias in their unique colouring of dusky apricot and tangerine, and even the orange daisies of the small and abundant ursinia. A gardener who thinks that annuals take too much of his time is not really interested in gardening. He is also missing the decoration which would look most conspicuous among the solid bones of bamboo and the features of vegetable leaves and grey senecio. Annuals are cheap, rewarding, quick and far more varied than growers of French marigolds imagine.

Wide glass windows in the sun room of the suburban garden give an excellent view of the massed plants.

Decoration was also meant to spill into our gravel surfacing. Gravel sharpens a garden's drainage, yet retains a cool moisture, as anyone who digs into a heap of gravel in summer will soon discover. Plants like it; when set in beds beside gravel paths, even the rare ones seed freely into the gravel's surface and root in surprisingly little earth. The gardener can encourage this. In his gravel he could plant thymes, soapwort, sandwort, the very smallest cotoneasters, sun roses, mints, bugle, golden marjoram, creeping jenny, and generous sweeps of self-sown erinus, that most prolific of 3in-high plants, which brightens up any wall or paved garden in late May with its small spikes of rose-red flowers. It would not matter if passers-by trod several of these plants to death. Every year, annual seeds could be broadcast from a packet so that patches come up to give summer colour. Fairy toadflax, small primrose eschscholzias, phacelias, night-scented stocks and mignonette would be more than able to cope with this treatment.

Decoration is not only confined to the gravel or the beds of annuals. The terrace and surrounds of the seat could also be varied and brightened with pot plants, tubs and flowering perennials. Here, the range of our town garden merges into the waterside terrace of our suburban garden.

Lapageria rosea.

THE SUBURBAN GARDEN

Planting for bones, feature and ornament is a principle which applies to any site or style. The same theory ran through our suburban garden whose bolder terrace suited a bolder use of decoration. Though many of its plants would also suit the paved areas of our town garden, their possibilities can be seen more clearly in the context of the larger, suburban site.

Through the wide glass windows of our sun room every gardener would want to see hanging climbers and sprawling plants which would be equally at home in a cold greenhouse or conservatory. Four plants are outstanding in such a situation. The sweet-scented white jasmine, *Jasminum polyanthum* bears white flowers from pinkish buds and is rampant if left to climb from a large pot. It is extremely sweet-scented, often being used as a hardy plant to spice small courtyards on Greek islands. The rarer *J. mesnyi* is also excellent, but its charm is colour, not scent. Its butter-yellow flowers are larger and rounded, opening in February, along most vigorous tendrils. The ice-blue *Plumbago capensis* is the finest accompaniment for conservatories in summer, a simple climber whose flowers can be picked and floated prettily in flat dishes of water. The very sweet-scented *Mandevilla suaveolens*, a climber from the Argentine, is too good to omit and although a rare plant it is most easily raised from seed. Its white flowers are shaped like small funnels and are borne in bunches between the leaves in late summer. The pink-flowered *Lapageria rosea* – after the maiden name of Napoleon's Empress Josephine – is a less vigorous companion, but perhaps it is the loveliest climber of all, especially on the shaded wall of a cool conservatory. Its hanging rose-pink flowers are so exotic that you will be proud to have ever helped them to appear.

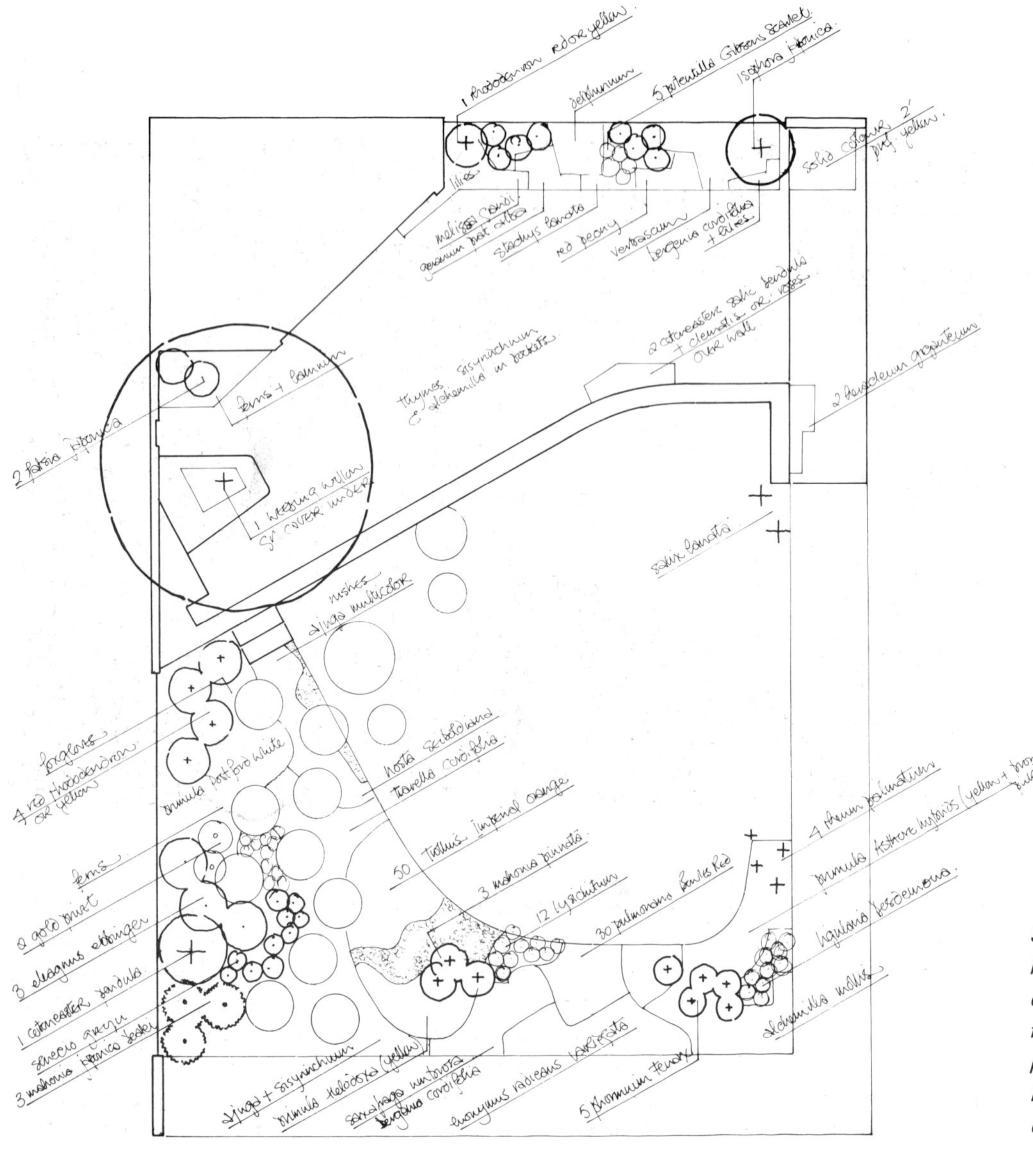

Suburban-garden planting plan. A large weeping willow balanced the sunroom/sculpture composition, with an herbaceous border on the far boundary flopping out on to the terrace. The planting surrounding the pool was of very broad bands of bright colour interlocking with cobbled areas running down by the edge.

red or yellow rhododendron
delphinium
Potentilla *'Gibson's Scarlet'*
Sophora japonica
solid colour, 2ft, preferably yellow
Melissa grandiflora
Geranium pratense alba
Stachys lanata
red paeony
Verbascum bombycifera
Bergenia cordifolia *plus lilies*
Heracleum giganteum
Cotoneaster salicifolia pendula *plus clematis or roses over wall*
thymes, sisyrinchium and alchemilla in pockets
ferns and lamium

Fatsia japonica
weeping willow with ground cover under rushes
rushes
Ajuga reptans
Hosta sieboldiana
Tiarella cordifolia
Trollius *'Imperial Orange'*
Mahonia pinnata
lysichitum
Pulmonaria *'Bowles Red'*
Rheum palmatum
Primula *'Ashore' hybrids (yellow and bronzy pink)*
Ligularia *'Desdemona'*
Alchemilla mollis
Phormium tenax

Euonymus radicans variegatus
Saxifraga umbrosa
Bergenia cordifolia
Primula helodoxa
Ajuga reptans *plus sisyrinchium*
Mahonia japonica
Senecio greyii
Cotoneaster salicifolia pendula
Elaeagnus ebbingei
gol privet
ferns
Primula *'Postford white'*
red or yellow rhododendron
foxgloves

The exotic white flowers of an angel's trumpet (datura).

These climbers are killed by frost, but are in no sense hot-house plants. They like a cool conservatory and, between November and May, they could be joined by pot-plants from the terrace outside. Many of the most decorative pot-plants are not certain to survive cold winters, so they should be brought indoors for shelter. I would not now have a terrace without a potted plant of *Abutilon vitifolium*, a quick-growing standard shrub whose saucer-shaped flowers of violet blue are a delight in May and June. The heavy-scented hanging trumpets of the white datura – an opulent and invaluable flower despite its coarse leaves – continue the terrace's season. I could not believe that these flowers, known as Angel's Trumpets, were real when I first saw them. They dangle downwards to a length of 9in and the mouths of their trumpets are closed with a crossed pattern of white petals. The grey-leaved *Helichrysum petiolatum* matches them pleasingly. It can be trained to grow rapidly over an arc of wires above a large pot where its refined and rounded leaves make up for the datura's coarseness. It can also be mixed among borders, annuals or beds of leaves and is easily perpetuated by cuttings wintered indoors. Lemon verbena is a pleasure for pinching; the tropical cactus-shaped leaves of cordylines are a contrast; the palm-like fans of dracaena suggest more tropical countries. All these could be enjoyed in pots on a sunny terrace and could be moved into the conservatory from October to May. Lilies would mix well in pots beside them and could be left outside all the year round, especially the selected forms of *L. auratum* whose huge flowers and strong scent enliven any August. They must have peat and no lime, a taste shared by *L. speciosum*, particularly in its lovely white form *album*. These two lilies are easily grown in pots, even in semi-shade; *L. speciosum* will multiply freely. Gardeners on limy soil can content themselves with the scent of *L. regale* which is so pleasant a month before its two late-summer

The exotic flower of Lilium auratum.

relations come into flower. There is no difficulty about growing a lily in a pot provided that the pot is deep enough for the stem-rooting kinds like *L. auratum*. Never give *L. regale* any manure as it can rot it to death.

Although scent is as much of an embellishment to the garden as it is to the face, these scented pot plants have such firm leaves that, if they were fully hardy, they would deserve to be placed as permanent bones. They were most appropriate for the suburban garden. Its mood was more modern and its features had been built as much as planted. Its bones, therefore, needed to suit a more architectural setting and to stand out more boldly, especially as they were to be viewed as part of a larger surrounding. In the smaller space of the town garden, profusion and informal planting were ends in themselves. The garden did not merge with a larger lawn, so the plants could spill informally from a formal design. This informal formality should be a principle whenever any enclosed space is to be planted. But the shapes of the suburban garden were strong and less orthodox; the bigger plantings would have seemed as confused as a summer hay-field unless they had had an exceptionally firm backbone to hold them together when not in flower. From a distance a few firm plants can concentrate the attention and save the eye from bewilderment. The more open and expansive your site, the firmer and fewer the bones of your planting must be. There are worse principles with which to begin the planting of a half-acre site.

Seventy years ago the gardener was more commonly compared with a painter, merging his drifts of colour in a style which would have done credit to Turner or Monet. Now it is more rewarding to compare him with an architect. The modern mood of the garden called for 'architectural' plants. Those of strong spiky outline, great height, huge leaves or ornamental stems are indeed an architectural parallel

A border of scented plants with strong leaves and outstanding flowers which reflect the modern, architectural approach of the garden.

to much of our modern building. Many of the best can be combined with an area of water, such as was featured below our terrace wall, but there are others which are happy in ordinary conditions.

Among architectural plants for more usual, dry sites none has been so favoured or popular as the yucca. This is too good a plant for any gardener to ignore. It could have been grouped in our town garden's gravel, potted up for its terrace or planted in a gap between its paving slabs. The terrace of the suburban garden could have used it too, either individually or in masses, for massed yuccas make up in spikes what they lose in outline. The popular name of this exotic plant is Adam's Needle – with whose leaves Adam could indeed have stitched his skirt of fig leaves. The leaves are as pointed as those of a giant cactus and I would be wary of placing them where small children might get poked in the eye. The grey-green leaves, up to 2ft long, are held stiffly, even in the kind called *Y. flaccida*. The huge heads of ivory-white bell-shaped flowers are without rival, though not produced unfailingly every year. A yucca is hardy, even on clay, but flowers most freely in warm gritty soil. Far the biggest is *Y. gloriosa*, which eventually reaches 6ft. This has the fault of becoming bare along its lower 2ft, thus looking ill at ease. Most gardeners would be better off with *Y. flaccida*, which is smaller, neater and rather more grey in leaf. *Y. filamentosa* has narrower leaves, more like a cordyline, and is good in its quieter way. When the ivory flowers appear, they can be studied for their hints of pale green and cream yellow. Their shading is very subtle.

Yuccas, then, on a modern terrace, and why not acanthus too? No plant has an older claim to be called architectural, as its leaves inspired Greek sculptors for their columns 2,000 years ago. Acanthus is slow to settle, then quick to spread. I like to mass its solid and spiny-leaved form, *A. spinosus*. Its vanilla-brown and white, hooded flowers are borne on 3ft stems and are viciously spined. I like these flowers because they are bold and unique, but the main interest of the acanthus is the leaf. In small spaces, the flowering stem could be removed so that the glossy, finely-cut leaves form a lower and neater clump. They are not quite evergreen as the frost usually removes them in late November, but they are quick to grow again in early spring and can be relied upon for at least an eight-month season. Those who like a flabby leaf, not a firm spiky one, would prefer *A. mollis* which has leaves of soft and squashy green. Most acanthuses are excellent; the choice depends on your taste, though there is not so much joy in a small form of *A. spinosus* listed as *A. caroli-alexandri*.

Not wishing to stress spikes and prickles too much, I must nonetheless put in a word for thistle plants. Perhaps these are not suitable for a terrace where yuccas, too, would make walking a dangerous business, but like an acanthus they can be prettily grouped in edges and corners or massed in flanking borders away from legs and feet. The taller eryngiums are worth hunting out. Far bolder than their small silvery relations, they are hardy plants with high and slender flower stems above strap-shaped clumps of leaves. The species called *E. serra* and *E. pandanifolium* are most impressive, though their toothed edges are not to be brushed without gloves.

The massive biennial onopordons or Scotch thistles are more familiar. These grow to look like a pewter candelabrum and reach a height of 7ft before bearing mauve thistle-flowers on their grey branches. Plant two of these, perhaps on either side of a modern conservatory, and they will dominate a whole corner of a garden.

If you think this idea is becoming too prickly, try the fan of stiff pointed leaves borne by the giant montbretia, *Curtonus paniculatus* – a neglected hardy plant which is most architectural. The long pointed leaves of *Phormium tenax*, the New Zealand flax, are magnificent, though not always hardy. Fill in around them with the largest tobacco plant, *Nicotiana silvestris*, whose long green leaves do

Left: *the huge* Yucca gloriosa.

A dominating plant, the Scotch thistle, Onopordon arabicum.

Nicotiana silvestris, *the largest tobacco plant.*

Essential by water, a form of rhubarb, Rheum palmatum purpurea.

resemble those found in a true tobacco plantation. Its small and hanging tubular flowers are white, scented and borne on sticky 4ft long stems. The fuzz of fennel could accompany it, especially in a dark-leaved form, such as 'Black Knight'. Fennel sprouts plumes in spring which are compact and most attractive. These then grow into waving stems in summer, topped by the flat heads of greenish yellow flower. I do not much like its smell and its habit of seeding indiscriminately, but its beautiful dark and feathery effect is only matched on a smaller scale by the white clouds of flower on a gypsophila.

Down by our pond the backbone to the planting would not need to consider such thorns or thistles. Five water plants stand out for their gigantic leaves, and I would never plant a pond without at least four of them. The first—a form of rhubarb (*Rheum palmatum*) in its red-leaved variety—flourishes in a deep soil and does not insist on waterside conditions for its lush leaves. I have grown it in a sunny

Gunnera manicata *in moisture garden with bergenias and grasses.*

border, but it is never so fine as in a damp water-bed where its wine-flushed leaves stand up thickly and firmly like those of a stiffened rhubarb. Its tall flower spike looks rather naked above these leaves, but I suppose it could be called architectural too. A more pleasing season for this rhubarb is early spring when its leaves begin to sprout, blood-purple and crinkled like those on a young beetroot.

Rhubarb is shamed, however, by the giant of all water plants, the Brazilian *Gunnera manicata*. One plant of this goes a long way – to some 15ft of mature span. I cannot pretend this is a small garden's backbone, though a plan could be composed around only one specimen. In winter, it is asleep and only shows pink brown buds above ground. In March its first leaves spring up, often to be frosted so that they lag behind its weird apologies for flowers. These look like a huge cone dropped from an excessively sappy fir. In early summer the leaves race ahead on thick prickly stems and open out like the leaves on a scalloped rhubarb plant. Their width, however, is as huge as 5ft and they are strutted with broad veins. Looking like a titanic umbrella, it is the most startling bone for a bold gardener and really quite obliging in sites which are not too frosty. In November the gunnera's leaves wither and rot; they are a curiously melancholy sight as they crumple forward in sad decay. The plant must then be tucked up for the winter. The old leaves are packed like a blanket over the plant's crown and held down by wire netting. This covering is not pretty, especially as gunnera's girth is so huge. I am told that one expert lover of gunneras even wraps his plant in an old dog blanket. No garden with a sizeable sheet of water should be without this king of all architectural plants beside it for the pleasure of the reflections and play of light upon its leaves.

Ligularia sounds sinister, but is far more amenable. Every small water garden needs this plant. It is unmistakable with its smooth, rounded leaves and its daisy flowers of pure glowing orange. The form called *L. clivorum* 'Desdemona' is quite comfortably the best. Its leaves, almost as striking as those in a form called *L. hessei*, are a purple green both above and below, set off by very free stems of flower. This plant has to have a damp soil, hence its use by the waterside where the pond's water would flood over any adjoining bed and keep it wet. Peat, manure and leaf-mould belong with this preference.

The same surroundings suit a glossier plant, *Peltiphyllum peltatum*, or water saxifrage. Away from a wet soil this looks miserable and shows brown marks over its umbrella-like leaves, but near the water's edge it is invaluable. Before the leaves shoot up, it bears pretty pink flower-heads, a relief from the yellows which otherwise dominate bog-gardens in spring. It makes a thick mat of roots, then shades them during summer with its handsome and shining leaves, up to 1ft wide. These are its main attraction to my eye. I would use it as one of the masses to hold my water-garden together, balancing it with the more familiar rodgersia, a plant of more variety and emphasis than any other bone for a damp flower-bed.

Rodgersias are not evergreen, yet their strong mat of roots will keep out weeds throughout the year. Their fresh young leaves open out in spring, often at risk to a late frost which will blacken them. If they survive they spread into large and contrasting shapes, as lush as the damp in their bed allows. They hate to dry out. The two with the finest leaves will seldom flower, but a rodgersia's flower is off-white and fluffy like a large astilbe's so this is no serious loss. The species *R. aesculifolia* is my favourite, for its leaves are like those on a large horse chestnut, the tree from which it takes its name. *R. tabularis* is almost its equal. Its leaves are wider and rounder, and are sometimes bronzed along their indented edges. A group of three will hold together the smaller plantings round it.

A water garden is the site for small plantings of brightly coloured flowers, always more popular than leaves. Primulas spring to everybody's mind, and there are few brighter flowers for May than those to

Right: *the country garden.* Azalea ponticum, *the white azalea 'Palestrina' and* Rosa hugonis *'Canary Bird' ramping through the terrace balustrading.*

The stretch of water is held together with plant masses and the large grouped stones.

Left: *the central feature of the country garden was a wooden bench seat surrounding an old double-stemmed rhododendron from Exbury. The paving is of old York stone with an infilling of brick.*

Unlike other primulas, Primula vialii *with its poker-shaped flowers.*

Left: *a quiet seat in a corner of the country garden, with bluebells, the white azalea 'Palestrina' and lilies.*

be found in a mass of *Primula japonica*'s many forms. Their tiers of flower are borne on stiff stems above large crimped leaves. 'Miller's Crimson' and 'Postford White' are admirable forms for large plantings. Mauve is best enjoyed from *P. denticulata* – to my eye a more awkward ball of flower. The vicious pink of the small *P. rosea* must be placed discreetly, more so than the flame shades in the Lissadel Hybrids or the brick orange of the easy *P. bulleyana*. The rose-mauve flowers of *P. vialii* must stand by themselves, but deserve a bed of their own as they are shaped like a poker and look quite unlike any other primula. Try to plant primulas where they will be neither flooded nor parched. This is not an easy requirement, even beside a pond.

These bright primulas raise the question of colour, always a difficulty in the choice of decorations for a garden. Often too many colours are spotted together in small groups. Here, above all, a gardener must

The striped leaves of Iris pallida variegata *help bind together flower colours.*

The day-lily, Hemerocallis *'Blushing Belle'.*

Alchemilla mollis *retains its green foliage for eight months of the year.*

Lysichitum americanum.

be restrained and thoughtful. As with the bones and features, colour needs a theme. Two perhaps can dominate, linked by their intermediate shades. No garden is too small for this principle, and for our spring planting we chose green and yellow.

The colours of the flowers could be neatly linked by the stripes and markings of variegated leaves. We used the variegated irises – *Iris pallida* and *I. kaempferi* – for the waterside. The yellow and white marks on their fresh green leaves could be matched with the yellow variegated form of Solomon's seal, the bright gold leaf of the meadow-sweet *Filipendula ulmaria aurea* or that of an orange blossom, *Philadelphus coronarius aureus*, which also likes damp soil. Hostas would be equally suitable.

Such green and gold leaves are a neat companion for green and golden flowers. The rampant acid-green flowers of lady's mantle (*Alchemilla mollis*); some of the smaller spurges, like *Euphorbia cyparissias* and *E. polychroma*; green-flowered *Heuchera* 'Greenfinch', and the green-white astrantias of alpine meadows could combine with the brighter golds and yellows of a day-lily, such as *Hemerocallis* 'Hyperion' or 'Golden Belle'; brilliant yellow *Lysichitum; Trollius*, the globe flower, in all its admirable forms for any damp site; gay yellow kingcups (*Caltha palustris*); the double buttercups of *Ranunculus acris plenus*; and the elegant lemon-yellow flowers of *Kirengeshoma palmata* which look like shuttlecocks. With all these can be grown the full range of water irises, especially *I. sibirica*. Grasses could be mixed among them in moderation, especially the small golden *Milium effusum aureum* and the variegated forms of *Glyceria*, which like water and are marked with pink and white. But when a dominant pattern of colour has been chosen, it must not be lost among too many varieties, otherwise the garden's decoration will become a confused muddle.

THE COUNTRY GARDEN

Colour was one of the main threads which led us into the design of our country garden. Here we moved still farther away from formality, though the principle of bones, features and decoration stayed with us throughout, and ended on the edge of a wild garden. The central area might indeed have been a natural dell of grass in a proper wilderness. No style of gardening is more difficult to plant successfully. The planning of colours is one basis from which to start.

Along the rise and fall of the bank on the garden's left side we planted mixed hybrid azaleas, trying to blend their colours to suit a natural wilderness. Here, it helps to remember that pinks, reds, yellows and oranges are social colours, whereas white and blues are sterner and less easily graded. The effects of light and shade should also be considered. White will look its best in a darker position, as will the fresh spring greens and yellows, as in our suburban garden. Dark red will show up clearly in sunlight against a glossy evergreen or beside a mass of silver leaves, a happy accompaniment, too, for all blues. Always distinguish between true blue and nurseryman's blue, which is more often a purple or mauve. Remember the many gradations of pink and purple – magenta, for instance, will combine with a dark red, not with a salmon pink. Rose pink will match mauve, not scarlet. It is a romantic fallacy that the natural colours of plants will never clash. A family like the rhododendron ranges through all the shades from ruby to pale pink, so the colour must first be precisely described in your own mind, then sited and flanked most carefully. The placing of colours is all a matter of distinguishing nearby tones. More gardeners should make use of the Royal Horticultural Society's colour chart and much value can be gained from Edwardian books on flower colour, especially *Colour in the Garden* by Miss Jekyll. She was herself a painter by profession until her eyesight grew weak and she turned to gardening.

Right: *mixed hybrid azaleas, planted to resemble a natural wilderness.*

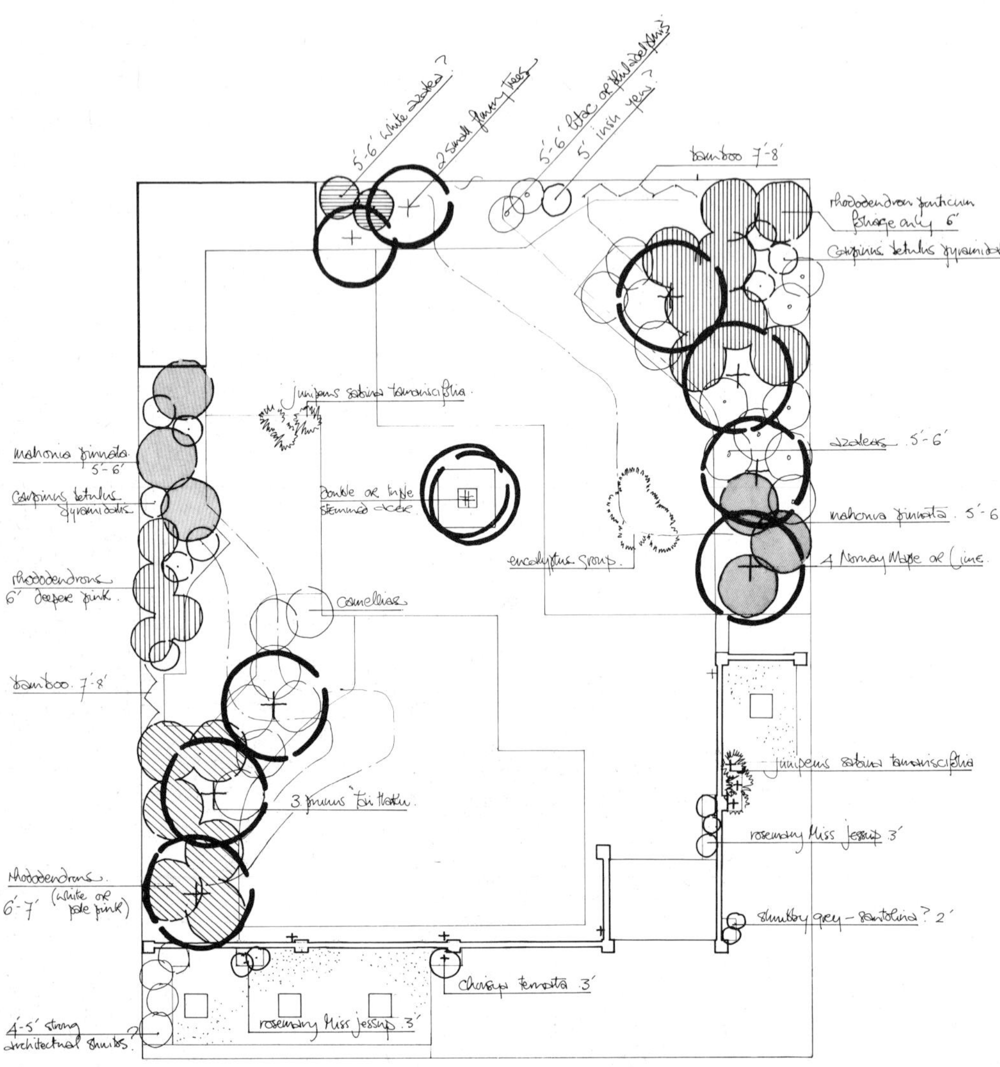

Country-garden planting plan. The shape of the garden ultimately changed (see constructional detail on page 44). Planting was to emphasise and build-up the contoured hillocks on either side with very soft foreground colour.

5–6ft Mahonia pinnata
Carpinus betulus *'Pyramidalis'*
6ft deep pink rhododendrons
7–8ft bamboo
6–7ft white or pale pink rhododendrons
4–5ft strong architectural shrubs
3ft rosemary 'Miss Jessop'
3 Prunus *'Tai Haku'*
camellias
Juniperus sabina tamariscifolia
double- or triple-stemmed acer
eucalyptus group

5–6ft white azaleas
2 small flowering trees
5–6ft lilac or philadelphus
5ft Irish yew
7–8ft bamboo
Rhododendron ponticum *foliage*
Carpinus betulus *'Pyramidalis'*
5–6ft azaleas
4 Norway maples or limes
Juniperus sabina tamariscifolia
Rosmarinus officinalis *'Miss Jessop's upright*
grey shrub (santolina)

We tried to mix our azaleas in the colours which go to make up a flame, separating the whites into darker or more isolated places. This grading is part of the planter's art. Never mix too closely deciduous azaleas with the harder shape and colours of the larger, evergreen rhododendron. For a natural drift or a wild planting on acid soil, the azalea is invaluable – a first choice where the bulkier mass and duller leaf of most rhododendrons would look incongruous. Our azaleas were mostly Exbury Hybrids, and we were fortunate in some splendidly mature plants of the white variety, 'Palestrina'. We massed these with a blue comfrey and thus kept the harder colours apart. The gradations of colour in a flame can be enjoyed by gardeners willing to combine the best Knap Hill and Ghent hybrid azaleas, especially as the Ghent crosses flower later in the season. 'Harvest Moon', a lemon yellow, could merge into 'Lapwing', a pale yellow tinged with pink and marked with orange; then into the early 'Golden Oriole'; then the butter-yellow 'Sun Chariot'; then the deep orange 'Hugh Wormald'; and then 'Speks Brilliant', the strongest orange red which is also marked with yellow. This strong colour could stand at the centre of the group, graded into the distance by a repeated sequence of the same lesser yellows. These Knap Hill Hybrids could be mixed, too, with the gay orange Ghent called 'Daybreak' and the pale yellow double 'Narcissiflora . Ghents have smaller flowers and a later season, but they also smell very sweetly.

In a wild country setting the principle of bones and decoration can be extended to a wider principle of layers. The planter should plan like nature, choosing his trees not only as his garden's bones but also as its top canopy. Beneath them lies the middle layer of wild shrubs, then comes the decoration of smaller herbaceous plants, and the plants to cover the ground, themselves a feature. Beneath them all come the bulbs, another decoration. The upper layers drop leaves on to the lower, sustaining their soil with leaf-mould. No gardening is ever free of trouble but this wild gardening, if properly planned, is reasonably easy to maintain.

Birches, poplars or even beeches should be avoided for the top layer as their roots are too ravenous to be interplanted with shrubs and bulbs. The plane tree is unsuitable as its leaves do not readily rot down into leaf-mould. The neglected and fast-growing larch, though greedy, can be excellent where a small copse is needed quickly. An attractive choice would be the Japanese *Larix leptolepis* whose twigs, coloured red-brown during winter, are most conspicuous. Limes are unsatisfactory. They are prone to aphids and drip black 'honeydew' off their leaves, and also drug bees with their narcotic flowers, causing them to lie dazed beneath their branches. The one faultless lime, *Tilia oliveri*, is very rarely available. We also used whitebeams, as in the town garden; a canopy of these would be most impressive, especially in late spring. The new leaves on a variety called *Sorbus aria lutescens* open out into a glistening grey from their winter buds, only later fading to a dark green. This whitebeam would have to be widely spaced as it is a broad-headed tree. Its leaves are not quick to rot into compost, but their spring display is too lovely to miss. Smaller gardens can enjoy the shorter, upright *Sorbus thuringiaca*, a fastigiate form.

Among smaller trees, the maple is my favourite canopy for a country wilderness. The autumn yellows of the quick-growing sugar maple, *Acer saccharinum*, are as pleasant as its lobed leaves, but it eventually becomes a very tall tree. The striped barks of the so-called snakebarks – *Acer davidii*, *A. pennsylvanicum* or *A. capillipes* – are most unusual and become more obvious as their trunks age. The

The layers of a garden with large shrubs surmounting the border plants which, in turn, give way to bulbs.

Acer hersii, *a form of maple well known for its snake-like bark.*

common field maple, *A. campestre*, is not to be despised as a round-headed feature which will grow happily on chalk or against wind. These are all satisfactory trees for underplanting, more so than the common sycamore which seeds far too copiously to be tolerated.

Beneath this canopy the gardener, on acid soil, would copy our azaleas and camellias, grading the latter from the white 'Alba Simplex' through the pale dawn-pink 'J. C. Williams' hybrid to the rose-pink 'Gloire de Nantes' and the scarlet 'Childsii' (or 'Rosette'), which could serve as the strong central colour. The witch hazel, slow but very free-flowering in its youth, would enjoy this lime-free soil, especially in its pale form called *Hamamelis mollis pallida*, the finest for the garden. It is most surprising that the witch hazel's petals, though thin as ribbon, are undamaged by frost.

There would be room for the informal lacecap hydrangeas, such as 'Blue Wave' and 'Lanarth White',

Hamamelis mollis, *the witch hazel, likes lime-free soil.*

so much more relaxed than the usual mop-heads, which would look far too formal for a country wilderness. The primrose bell-flowers of the lovely *Corylopsis pauciflora* could be set off by drifts of the smaller skimmias, those fragrant white-flowered evergreens which I prize for their fresh leaf and red berries, borne when two sexes meet on their respective plants. Skimmias can be increased with surprising facility from cuttings. The smaller bush maples could also stand at emphatic points, especially *A. palmatum* 'Senkaki' whose coral twigs in winter and yellow leaves in autumn are particularly gay. Except for skimmia and witch hazel, all these shrubs are happiest when sheltered from spring frost. A canopy of trees will help here too, for it is the aim of a wild garden that each layer should protect the one below it.

On limy soils gardeners have a harder time. The early primrose flowers of the wide-spreading *Cornus*

The gay yellow leaves of Acer palmatum *'Senkaki'.*

mas distinguish this tough small tree and make it worthy of the larger wild garden. The bright scarlet stems of dogwood, such as *C. alba* 'Westonbirt', will brighten any wilderness in winter. It can be mixed with the yellow-stemmed form *flaviramea* and the wiry white stems of the rampant ghost bramble, *Rubus cockburnianus*. Wild roses, single flowered only, can look appropriate, especially the small pink-white flowers of *Rosa farreri*, the threepenny-bit rose, and the smaller thickets of *R. spinosissima*, the Scotch or Burnet rose which is at home on sandy soils and has many colour forms. Small willow bushes, such as *Salix wehrhahnii*, will please the patient gardener who masses them for their grey leaves and catkins. Best of all these tough flowering shrubs would be clumps of Japanese quince, or *Chaenomeles*, massed for a spring display, then drifts of white lilac and mock orange-blossom (*Philadelphus*). All grow in shade, as does the sweet yellow *Ribes aureum*, an unfamiliar flowering currant. On an open bank, such as ours at the show, the horizontal lines of the admirable low evergreen *Prunus laurocerasus* 'Otto Luyken' could be contrasted with a background line of the quick and obliging deciduous shrub *Rubus tridel* 'Benenden' whose large white flowers in late May fit any natural setting. It soon spreads its elegant leaves and stems to a height and width of 6ft or more. I wish it were planted instead of so much forsythia.

The lower layers of such a country garden must not look too formal or seem to be arranged as if in a flower bed. In its rural setting, wild flowers would look both appropriate and plausible. Country gardening is ruined by the exotic or the alien, however lovely these may be elsewhere. Rhododendrons in a flat plain of limestone look as bizarre as box edged beds on a Scottish hillside. A planting which merges with its natural surroundings should observe their qualities before all else. Begin with the clues which your landscape gives you.

Rubus cockburnianus *with its wiry white stems.*

The Japanese quince, Chaenomeles speciosa.

A preferable alternative to forsythia? The white-flowered deciduous shrub Rubus tridel *'Benenden'.*

For those with land in the country this colourful meadow shows attractive naturalised planting of bluebells, buttercups and Saxifraga granulata.

Improved forms of wild flowers can be enjoyed at all levels. Creeping jenny, for example, makes a moderately vigorous carpet in damp and shaded places, even under trees. It is only an inch or two high, but if you choose the golden-leaved variety, *Lysimachia nummularia aurea*, you can bring light into a dark corner with a mass of its bright yellow leaves. The sweet woodruff, *Asperula odorata*, which flowered in time for our show garden, is another small native carpeter for informal planting. It also thrives in towns where it could be used instead of grass for a shaded lawn. Its small white flowers, smelling of mown hay, are set off prettily by its dark green leaves, though they are deciduous. London pride and Solomon's seal, especially in their variegated forms, will mix plausibly with such natives, as will lily-of-the-valley, a plant for carpets under trees. Forms of the wild fumitory are a more delicate companion. *Corydalis lutea* is prepared to spread freely, and its grey-green fern-like leaves are too beautiful to miss in a wild planting. The yellow flowers, resembling a bird's crest, can be combined with the pink-mauve *C. rubra* and a dark maroon form of *C. laciniata*. I do not object to the mixing of different coloured forms of the same plant, provided that this is done generously and the colours are a sensible match.

The most useful wild flower for such plantings is surely the cranesbill. Its stronger forms spread anywhere and their neat leaves often turn a bright red-orange before dying away in autumn. Some are aromatic and all bear graceful flowers. The cranesbill is the true geranium – so-called from the Greek word *geranos*, a crane whose bill the flower's seed-pods were thought to resemble. Foreign brothers of the meadow cranesbill (*Geranium pratense*) are perhaps the most easily placed. The invaluable *G. macrorrhizum* will grow more loosely in shade than in sun, but always makes a wide mat of aromatic leaves which bear single flowers of varying shades of pink. This can be left to pour under the branches of your shrubs, and the witch hazels or azaleas of your wilderness. It will grow on a bank, in dry shade or in poor town earth. The two finest forms are *album*, a grey-white, and Ingwersen's variety, a larger rose pink perhaps more suitable for a formal border. A very pretty variegated form is sometimes available. *Album*, the white form of *G. sylvaticum* – meaning 'cranesbill of the woods' – flowers sooner, in late May, and grows taller. It should be grouped in any glade or country planting and enjoys shade. It also comes in a pale violet colour in the form called 'Mayflower'. Many praise the varieties of *G. endressii*, but to me the only merit of their sickly pink flowers is that they will grow in the darkest shade.

The theme of wild flowers for a wild garden could be continued through hellebores, especially the winter-flowering green *Helleborus foetidus*; the perennial forget-me-not, *Brunnera macrophylla*; the white forms of lady's smock, *Cardamine pratensis*; traveller's joy (*Clematis vitalba*) grown as a creeper; primroses; cowslips; and forms of the spindle tree (*Euonymus*) which give fine autumn colour and can be pruned hard to keep them below 4ft. Ferns could be included, especially *Dryopteris*, the oak fern; also dark Irish ivy; tall loosestrife (*Lysimachia punctata*); Solomon's seal; sweet rocket (*Hesperis matronalis*), and the mats of *Dryas octopetala*, or Mountain Avens, which suit a peaty moorland. Please be very sure that you like heathers and that they suit your local landscape before you plant them in drifts. I have no wish to see them in my garden, not least because of their hideous leaves. I would prefer the bright blue forms of comfrey (*Symphytum*), one of which was massed most effectively among our white azaleas. *S. peregrinum* has sky-blue flowers and *S. caucasicum* deep blue, both of which open from pinkish buds. I prefer the latter form as its leaves are less coarse and it does not grow too tall. These comfreys will grow almost anywhere and will withstand a scything in long grass during the summer. So too will the foxglove, another essential feature for such a planting.

Left: Primula bulleyana *and digitalis (foxglove).*

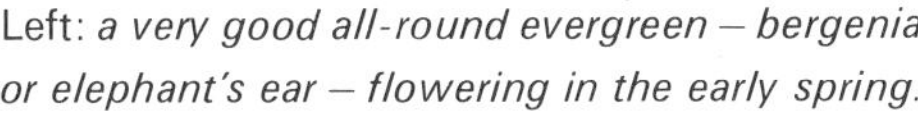

Left: *a very good all-round evergreen – bergenia or elephant's ear – flowering in the early spring.*

An arched yew hedge forming a frame for the tree beyond.

The winter-flowering Helleborus foetidus.

Clematis vitalba *with fruits, living up to its common name of old man's beard.*

Right: Anemone blanda *naturalised in grass.*

The beautifully-patterned flower of the snakeshead fritillary, Fritillaria meleagris.

The lowest layer of a wilderness and its main decoration are the bulbs. Aconites and snowdrops begin the year, followed by crocuses, especially forms of the wild species. The more usual fat hybrids of mauve, white and orange do not suit an informal setting and should be avoided. Among the species, *Crocus ancyrensis, C. chrysanthus, C. tomasinianus* and *C. biflorus* (the Scots' crocus) are the most obliging. Their forms come in many shades of colour. I would choose 'E. A. Bowles' as my yellow, *C. ancyrensis* as my orange, 'Blue Pearl' as my pale violet, and *C. biflorus albus* as my white. The wild forms of daffodil could accompany them, especially the Lent lily (*Narcissus pseudonarcissus*) and the Tenby daffodil (*N. obvallaris*). These small daffodils grow freely and in a grass wilderness will look far more appropriate than the long-stemmed hybrid narcissi or the strong yellows of 'King Alfred' or 'Golden Harvest' daffodils. Another wild flower, the snakeshead fritillary (*Fritillaria meleagris*)

would spread itself on any soil which was not too dry. This fritillary is the most beautiful bulb for any wild garden, though the smaller forms of anemone may surpass it in a massed show of colour. *Anemone blanda* is the finest; it is cheap, low-growing, quick to spread and gaily coloured when bearing its violet, white and rose-pink flowers in April. These open wide like daisies when the sun shines. They are most appropriate in any wild surroundings and are particularly happy on sandy soils.

From garden to garden, therefore, our planting varied but the principle of bones, features and decoration ran through all three. The town garden was a home for annuals and carpeting plants which decorated the gravel bones of the design. The suburban garden made room for a tapestry of small plants by the waterside, arranged mostly in greens and yellows. The country garden allowed for a groundwork of bulbs and wild carpeting plants among its informally massed shrubs. If they had sufficient space, gardeners might try to combine the decorations of all three. However, we learnt that it is important to select a theme and to garden strictly round it, planning the evergreen bones as a framework for a few repeated main features. A garden should be planted to suit its surroundings. No single setting suits every possible plant. The planter who tries to include every sort of flower may enjoy his wide collection, but he will not have produced a satisfactory garden. He will find that collections always need attention, for their needs differ as widely as the plants. A well-planned garden can be maintained more simply, not least because it has been planted round a repeated theme.

Part 3

Maintenance

by Arthur Hellyer

Many years ago, when a young friend of mine, a professional gardener, acquired his first small house he promptly covered the garden with asphalt. He had, he declared, quite enough hard work in his nursery and no intention of continuing it at home. Today he would have no such problem, for science and technology have greatly lightened the labour of maintaining a healthy weed-free garden. Fertilisers are no longer dusty and unpleasant to handle, and efficient distributors are available for both large and small areas. The weed problem has largely been solved by the development of new herbicides; some of these are highly selective in the plants they kill, while others by the use of special applicators can be directed accurately where they are required and nowhere else.

Nowadays small power-operated grass cutters are so cheap and efficient that they are rapidly replacing hand-operated machines which, perhaps, will soon be used only for certain specialist purposes. Easily manoeuvrable cultivators are available, also mini-tractors capable of tackling many different jobs, though these are implements for the larger garden where they may well take over the work of several gardeners. Hedge trimming, once a major operation, can now be completed quickly and easily with mechanical trimmers; some of these work off self-contained lightweight batteries which can be recharged when not in use. Small wonder that well-shaped hedges and topiary are coming back into fashion when they can be cared for so easily. Watering devices have also been marvellously improved and some can be made entirely automatic and independent of the gardener except for occasional inspection and adjustment. By the use of dilutors connected to the water supply it is possible to feed plants while they are being watered; this not only saves time but, under some circumstances, gives markedly better results than feeding via the soil.

Even the chemicals with which pests and diseases are controlled have been given a longer life so that it is not necessary to apply them so frequently. Spraying machines have been made lighter and more efficient, some models being power-operated like lightweight hedge trimmers.

Today's small cultivators can tackle difficult heavy jobs in large gardens.

But all these technological advances, beneficial though they may are, need to be used wisely and with understanding. I know many gardeners still buy mechanical tools that are unsuitable or underpowered for the work they will have to do and many use the wrong chemicals in the wrong way at the wrong time. It is horrifying to be told that old-fashioned sodium chlorate, one of the most dangerous of herbicides, is still the best seller.

The purpose of this section is not only to resolve some of these problems and misconceptions but to enable people to derive the maximum

Above: *a mini-tractor takes the hard work out of deep digging large plots.*

Right: *this spade is useful for old people and the disabled as it eliminates stooping.*

pleasure from their gardens with the minimum degree of labour and error. It may be wise first to point out that bad design and preparation can make it impossible to get the best out of any of these modern aids. Awkwardly shaped lawns running right up to paths or walls will always be difficult to mow; plants that grow too large or too fast will involve extra work in restriction; soil that is badly prepared in the first instance can give rise to problems for many subsequent years. So, to ensure the maximum amount of relaxation is enjoyed from a garden, it is essential to consider from the outset all the interconnected possibilities of planning, planting and maintenance, which is why we have linked them together in this book.

GRASS

It is a widely held belief that grass is one of the easiest things to maintain and that when other garden features prove too time consuming the easy answer is to 'grass it over'. This is only partially true, a great deal depending on where the grass is and in what condition it is to be kept. A lawn was featured in our country garden, where we felt it was essential as a natural setting for the informal groupings of trees, shrubs and perennials. In towns, grass often suffers severely from lack of light and overwear, and under such conditions it may be necessary to re-sow each spring to maintain a worthwhile lawn. In such circumstances all thought of using a fine grass mixture of fescues and bent grasses (*agrostis* species) should be abandoned and the lawn be made with a leafy perennial rye grass or one of the good strains of smooth-stalked meadow grass (called 'Kentucky Blue' in America, where it is very popular), either of which will germinate quickly and give a good green cover in a few weeks.

Such grasses are useful in suburban and country gardens also, not for lawns that are to be close mown but for areas of coarser turf, cut to between 1 and 2in and used primarily as a green surround for trees, shrubs and flower borders. Good use can be made of the contrast in colour and texture of close-mown and long-mown grass, as can be observed on any golf course where, on greens, fairways and rough, three kinds of ground cover can be seen.

A neatly maintained lawn acts as an effective frame for this suburban house.

Mowing

This raises the question of how and when to mow. For the finest, closest finish there is still nothing to beat the traditional cylinder-type lawn mower, whether hand or power propelled. With this kind of machine the quality of finish will depend partly on the blades being kept sharp and well adjusted, but also on the number of cuts made in relation to the forward movement of the machine. This is always expressed as 'cuts per yard' and the very finest machines, as used for bowling and putting greens, may give 130 cuts per yard or even more. Contrast this with rough-cut machines giving perhaps twenty-five cuts per yard and it will be seen what a range there is. A high rate of cutting is achieved partly by higher gearing of the cutting 'cylinder' and partly by increasing the number of blades on the cylinder, which may have anything from three to eight. However, it is fairly obvious that the higher the rate of cutting the greater the amount of work being done. With power-operated machines this is not very important since manufacturers will take care of it by fitting a more powerful engine, but if the machine is hand propelled it is a point that must be considered carefully. Only a fairly robust gardener will want to push a machine giving sixty cuts per yard, about the lowest rate for really fine playing surfaces. Much less energy is required to propel a machine giving around forty-five cuts per yard, and provided it is maintained in good condition this will give a very good-looking finish.

All this is based on the assumption that wheels and cutting blades are geared together. On some small machines a motor is provided simply to drive the blades and the wheels are free, their purpose being to allow the machine to be pushed over the grass at any desired speed. With such machines the slower one walks the more cuts one gets per yard and actually with less effort. Machines of this type are usually electrically powered, either from a battery or from a mains supply by way of a long cable. They have become very popular for small lawns, but are not, in general, sufficiently large or robustly constructed to be recommended for extensive ones.

The bigger power-driven machines fall into four categories: cylinder (already described), rotary, flail and sickle-bar.

Rotary mowers do not cut with a scissor action like cylinder machines, but by slashing the grass as with a sickle or scythe. They are much better able to deal with grass that is long or very wet, but even the best of them do not produce quite the superb finish that can be obtained with a high-class cylinder machine.

All the same, rotary grass cutters are versatile. They can tackle the rough cutting just as easily as the light cutting, and their ability to work in the wet can be an immense advantage for anyone who can only garden at weekends or on occasional evenings. Because of these advantages, there is a lot to be said for having a rotary grass cutter at hand even if most of the mowing is done with a cylinder machine.

In trying to keep prices competitive, manufacturers of popular machines tend to fit engines that are only just adequate for their work. As they lose tune they may be only just able to carry on or may actually stall if the grass gets a little out of hand or is wet or unusually tough. So, if a choice is available, it is nearly always wise to choose the model with the most powerful engine for that particular cutting width. This is important if there is enough grass – say $\frac{1}{4}$ acre or more – to justify buying a ride-on grass cutter or one of the mini-tractors to which grass-cutting equipment can be attached. Where the area to be cut does not exceed $\frac{1}{2}$ acre and the grass is never likely to be very long or tough, a 5hp engine may be sufficient, though 7hp would almost certainly be better. But when one gets to paddock cutting and the like it is wise to buy in the 10–14hp range.

The air-cushion rotary mower is ideal for cutting grass under large shrubs.

The air-cushion rotary can be invaluable for cutting steep banks since it can be moved freely in any direction and swung along a bank from the top or even lowered down it on a rope. These mowers usually have no wheels and are fitted

An edge trimmer smartens lawns and cuts down on mowing time.

with very slim hoods, which act as a 'skirt' for the air cushion as well as a protection from the rotating blades. They can be slipped under low branches of trees, shrubs, etc, more easily than most mowers and are also useful for cutting along the edges of borders where plants overhang the turf.

Flail machines cut by means of small hinged blades mounted on a rotating cylinder. They slash off the grass, like a rotary, but throw it out backwards more or less evenly and do not collect it in swathes to one side as do most rotaries. This means that if the machine is not fitted with a pick-up box or sack it may be possible to let the cut grass lie, as a thin mulch which will wither away in a day or so; whereas the swathes left by rotaries look unsightly and may smother the grass underneath unless they are raked or swept up. Power-driven sweepers will deal with this problem, but their use means yet another job and further expense.

The sickle-bar mower or motor scythe makes use of a reciprocating bar carrying triangular blades – exactly the same principle as that used in farm hay cutters and reapers. Unlike all the others, which mince the grass up, making it unusable for anything except a mulch or the compost heap, this kind of machine will cut the longest grass cleanly. This can be an advantage if you want to make hay, a drawback if you want to let the grass lie and die. But no machine is more effective than this in dealing with really tall grass and weed, and in a big garden, where some areas can only be cut once or twice a year, it can be essential. In addition to being made as single-purpose machines, sickle-bar attachments are available for some mini-tractors.

Much mowing time will be saved if every area of turf has a clean cutting edge. This should either be a clear 1½in above any adjacent path or paved area or, if these must be level, a little gulley about 2in deep and 3in wide should be left between turf and paving. This will allow shears or a mechanical edge trimmer to be used easily, and the gulley itself can be kept weed-free by one treatment each spring with a persistent residual herbicide, such as simazine or dichlobenil.

Mowing problems can also be caused by taking grass too close to walls, fences and other obstructions. It is better to make a border in such a place or run a strip of paving sufficiently wide to permit a mower to be worked right up to and over the edge of the turf.

Weeds on Lawns

Wild flowers in rough-mown grass can look very attractive, but most people would agree they are out of place in a close-mown lawn. Here an unbroken carpet of green looks better, and weeds, which differ from the grass in colour, texture and rate of growth, must be eliminated as far as pos-

No weeds to spoil the surface of this attractive lawn.

sible. This is now much easier to do, thanks to the multiplication of selective herbicides. On lawns one obviously needs to use those that are relatively harmless to grass. I say 'relatively' advisedly since no herbicide is totally without effect on grass. Even the best will depress its growth and dull its colour temporarily, which is one good reason for not dosing lawns with selective weed killers unless they really need it. Since these chemicals kill weeds most effectively when they are in active growth, it is also a good idea to feed a lawn a few days before using weed-killer on it, since this makes the weeds more sensitive and helps the grass to grow quickly out of any check it may receive.

The lawn weed-killers most commonly used are 2,4-D, MCPA, mecoprop, fenoprop, dichlorprop, ioxynil and morphamquat. Ioxynil and morphamquat are particularly useful on young seedling grass which can be severely injured by some of the other herbicides, and are also effective against speedwells (veronica); 2,4-D and MCPA will kill many of the common lawn weeds but are of little use against clovers, medics, trefoils or yarrow, which is where mecoprop, fenoprop and dichlorprop come in useful.

They are sold under trade names, often in mixtures of two or even three for a wider band of efficacy. The chemical ingredients will be given on the container, probably in small type. The best course is to pick a brand that includes chemicals effective against common weeds and clovers. Use it over the whole lawn area in April or May when grass is growing strongly and then, if necessary, spot-treat any weeds that appear during the summer. The herbicides can be purchased ready-mixed with fertiliser so that feeding and weed-killing can be done at one operation, or as concentrated liquids to be diluted with water and sprayed or watered on to the weeds.

Left: *pumping up a modern pneumatic sprayer.*

The quickest and safest method of doing this is to use a special applicator fitted with a sprinkle-bar which will deliver the diluted fluid at the correct rate if moved over the lawn at steady walking pace. For quick treatment of large surfaces, such as lawns and paths, one needs a long sprinkle-bar—say, anything from 1 to 2ft—whereas for weeds among growing plants one needs a short bar of about 3in. Most applicators are supplied with one of each.

Moss can be a problem, though it is one that is apt to come and go with the seasons without any action on the part of the gardener. When it proves more persistent and troublesome, it must be removed with one of the proprietary moss-killers usually based on sulphate of iron or on calomel. However, severe growth is usually an indication that something is wrong with the soil – maybe it has become very compacted so that the surface is moist but the soil below is dry; or it has become too acid, or is very deficient in plant food. Usually a little investigation will reveal which of these causes is the most likely, or that it is a combination of two or all three. Then appropriate action should be taken – spiking, followed by applications of coarse sand well brushed in to improve aeration and lower acidity, or fertiliser according to label instructions to increase soil fertility. Only in severe cases of acidity should lime be used on lawns.

Feeding and Watering

To be kept in good condition lawns need feeding every six or eight weeks from about mid-April until mid-August. Specially formulated lawn fertilisers may be used, but in most cases equally good results will be obtained more cheaply by using a well-balanced general fertiliser, such as National Growmore. 'Well balanced' means that it will contain approximately equal percentages

Right: *a rotary sprinkler.*
Below: *an oscillating sprinkler seen here in action.*

of nitrogen, phosphoric acid and potash (the National Growmore analysis is 7:7:7), but for lawns it will actually be an advantage if there is a slight excess of nitrogen. Whatever fertiliser is used it should be granular; this makes it much easier to apply evenly and without drifting where it is not wanted. Small spreaders are readily available, but I find it just as easy to scatter the fertiliser by hand.

Water is, if anything, even more essential than food. It may only be required for a few weeks each summer but lack of it can kill much of the grass and give clovers, medics and deep-rooted weeds a head start. The ideal is a sprinkler that will deliver about $\frac{1}{2}$in of water per hour; this fairly low rate of application gives the water time to soak in and the sprinkler can be left unattended for at least an hour while one gets on with some other job. Either rotating or oscillating spinklers will do, though the latter have a slight advantage in that they water a rectangle, not a circle, and so, when moved on, there need be little overlapping and consequent double watering.

The ultimate in labour saving is the pop-up sprinkler, which is fitted permanently in the lawn (as a rule it is necessary to have a battery of them spaced 30–100ft apart according to available pressure) sunk just below the level of the turf. When the water is turned on, the pressure forces each sprinkler up a couple of inches above the turf so that it can rotate and spray freely and, when the water is turned off, the sprinkler drops back into its socket again, virtually out of sight. Pop-up sprinkler installations are there permanently for instant use, either manually by turning a cock or automatically by means of a time switch and solenoid valve.

Mowers of all types can pass over them and the only kind of lawn operations with which they

An effective spiking implement for lawns made on heavy soils.

A portable spray unit for applying herbicides, pesticides and liquid fertilisers.

Right: *the purple and cream leaves of* Rheum palmatum *make a lovely foil to the sheet of water beyond.*

might interfere are spiking and slitting. How necessary these operations are depends upon the soil, the amount of wear the lawn gets and to some extent on the mowing policy adopted. It is when soils become compacted because they are naturally wet, sticky or heavily used that they need to be opened up again by spiking, and it is when a deep mat of dead grass and other rubbish forms beneath the sward that it must be torn out by slitting. Either operation can be carried out with simple hand tools, but it can be quite laborious work and if much of it has to be done it will almost certainly be wise to purchase or hire a power-driven machine. Many home lawns on good soil, regularly mown, fed and watered and occasionally raked and brushed, continue in good condition for years without any need for spiking or slitting.

Brushing is always good for lawns and can be done expeditiously with one of the rotary sweepers that are also so useful for picking up leaves in the autumn. These are available in a variety of sizes and models, including hand-propelled and power-driven machines. For the really well-equipped garden, there are outdoor vacuum sweepers.

PAVING AND GRAVEL

In our country garden we also used a lot of paving, both for the terrace at the house end and in a series of large interlocked rectangles giving firm, clean access to the thatched arbour at all seasons whatever the weather.

Though the maintenance of paved and gravelled areas is minimal, it is not entirely non-existent. Even when paving slabs are laid in concrete, some weeds will succeed in finding cracks in which to grow. In much of our paving, the crevices between slabs were deliberately left open so that creeping plants could be grown in them and, in our town garden, we even introduced such plants to the gravelled panels to soften the effect. Where plants can grow, weeds are certainly likely to appear.

Gravel may be loose or binding. We used both types and believe that both have their place in garden design. Loose gravel must be raked occasionally to maintain its particular gritty visual quality, and this raking will itself tend to dispose of many weeds while they are still too small to have much roothold. But some will survive and these, like those in hard rolled gravel or in paving, must be destroyed. It can, of course, be done by grubbing them out individually, but that is a slow job and some of the more firmly rooted ones will almost certainly be broken off and sprout half a dozen heads where before there was only one.

A better way is to treat each individually with a total herbicide, not a selective one, since it can in effect be made selective by applying it direct to the weed and to nothing else. The best chemicals for this purpose are simazine, paraquat, diquat and dichlobenil. Simazine remains in the surface soil for many months, inhibiting fresh growth, but it is not very speedy in killing weeds already there. Dichlobenil is very similar in its action, long lasting but slow starting. By contrast, paraquat and diquat will begin to blacken leaves in a few hours if the weather is warm and sunny. (They are not themselves plant poisons, but are converted into poisons by the chlorophyll in the leaves in the presence of sunlight). So a mixture of the two types of chemical – residual and contact – will give the best result. No such mixture with dichlobenil is offered, this chemical being marketed as a fine powder in a special dispenser which enables it to be sprinkled just where it is required. It is very convenient and very effective, but one must be prepared to wait a few weeks for results.

Mixtures of simazine and paraquat are available ready for dissolving in water and application to the weeds – preferably from a special applicator fitted with the shortest of sprinkle-bars so that the liquid can be directed precisely where it is required and nowhere else. Remem-

Opposite.
Top: Laburnum waterii vossii.
Bottom: *ceanothus can be grown either on a wall or more usually as a shrub. There are both evergreen and deciduous types – the latter being not quite so hardy.*

ber that these chemicals do not distinguish between garden plants and weeds, but will kill both if they come in contact with them. There is no danger if they are applied only to the weeds, since paraquat can only act through leaves and simazine moves very little in the soil.

Finally, with paving of all kinds, including bricks, the presence of green slime can be unsightly and in wet weather can become dangerously slippery. A simple remedy is to wet or scrub with salt water (about 4oz common salt in each gallon of water). Care must be taken to keep this off plants, for salt is also a herbicide and since it is very soluble it can be carried for considerable distances in the soil. So only the minimum amount of fluid should be used and it should not be splashed about indiscriminately.

Since the scum is caused by the growth of algae, a more sophisticated remedy is to water or spray with an algicide – a chemical specially potent against them. The most widely available has the unfortunate chemical name alkyldimethylbenzyl ammonium chloride, but it is marketed under the trade name Dimanin. One pack of this makes 2gal of wash which can be applied to the scummy paving with a paint brush or scrubbing brush.

There remains the care of any plants grown in the paving or gravel. Provided they have been properly chosen, they will require no feeding or transplanting, and only an occasional trimming with shears or scissors if they spread too far;

The Chelsea town garden was based on a judicious mixture of paving, bricks and gravel, the textures contouring in a harmonious whole.

Left: *the country garden with plant groups interspersed in the paved area to break up the somewhat severe lines of the slabs.*

this can be done at any time in spring or summer though the most favourable time is usually immediately after flowering.

BEDS AND BORDERS

Only ground used for vegetables or for strictly temporary ornamentals, such as annuals and bedding plants, should be regularly dug or forked. For all the more permanent plants, such as trees, shrubs, roses and perennials, any deep cultivation once they have been planted can only do harm by destroying the roots that grow near the surface where the soil is nearly always more fertile. The most that should be done is to loosen the surface 1–2in deep with a fork to work in top dressings of manure, compost or fertiliser, but it is usually just as effective and less dangerous to leave them to be washed in by rain or pulled in by worms.

The age-old problem of weeds and the general desire for tidiness would, until recently have been entirely a matter of hoeing, and the hoe, provided it is used lightly, is still a useful tool for surface cultivation and weed killing. But hoeing takes time and is not effective against weeds that grow readily from severed roots. So the modern alternatives of peat mulch and herbicide application are worth careful attention.

Mulching

The idea of the peat mulch is to cover the surface with a $\frac{1}{2}$–1in layer of loose peat which will discourage seeds from germinating and make it easy to pull or hoe them out if they do grow. It can even be quite an effective counter to some creeping weeds, such as sheeps sorrel and ground elder, which are difficult to eradicate with herbicides. Such weeds tend to grow up into the loose mulch from which it is fairly easy to drag them with all their roots, whereas in the more consolidated soil below they would tend to break off, leaving roots to produce new and even more numerous plants.

Above: *mulching a young tree with rotted compost or manure.*

Peat for mulching can be of almost any kind, sedge or sphagnum, fine or coarse. Some people think that sedge peat has a better appearance, others that sphagnum, being less decayed, lasts longer and so is more economical. There is something to be said on both sides. The one essential is that the peat should not be too acid unless it is to be used for really acid-loving plants, such as most rhododendrons and some heathers, or to lower the pH of very alkaline soil. It must also be moist, for dry peat repels water and can insulate the soil from light rainfall. It is most economically purchased in large polythene bales. Before use these should be stood on end, opened at the top and have several gallons of water poured into them, after which they should be left for a few hours so that the water can soak right through the peat. Alternatively the peat can be spread out on a hard surface, watered and thrown into a heap, which again should be left for a few hours so that the water really soaks in, moistening the peat evenly right through.

The main mulch should be spread in spring when the soil is still moist from winter rain. Subsequently it will be reduced gradually by decay, so to maintain the minimum effective thickness of about $\frac{1}{2}$in it will need to be topped up occasionally with more moist peat; the best time to do this is after rain or watering, so that there is no dry layer to impede the free passage of moisture.

Herbicides

The herbicides suitable for use on cultivated ground are much the same as those recommen-

Left: *an attractive border, free from weeds, using space on different levels with tiered shrubs and plants.*

ded for paving and gravel, but may need to be used at lower concentrations and certainly with even greater care. Unlike lawns where the plants to be retained – the grasses – are all of one kind and it is therefore possible to find a chemical that will not do them any serious harm, in a border the plants one is seeking to preserve are likely to be so miscellaneous that it would be impracticable to find a herbicide harmless to all of them. So one must make the herbicide selective by the method of application, either using a dry powder, such as dichlobenil, dusted carefully on the weed leaves and on the bare soil, but equally carefully kept off the leaves of garden plants, or using liquid herbicides applied direct to weed leaves and bare soil by means of a properly stoppered applicator and a short sprinkle-bar. This is better than using an open watering can from which herbicide can all too easily be splashed on to plants if one makes a false step or tips the can too steeply.

Paraquat and diquat are two of the safest chemicals to use for this kind of weed killing among growing plants since both are inactivated by contact with the soil and are only effective when applied to leaves or green stems. So, provided one does not apply too much and takes care to keep the liquid off the leaves of garden plants, no unwanted damage is likely to occur. The drawback to paraquat and diquat is that they are purely contact herbicides. They will kill plants on which they have been watered or sprayed, but, unlike dichlobenil, they have no residual effect which would enable them to prevent fresh weed growth.

Simazine, by contrast, is highly residual and may inhibit seedling growth for up to a year. It is widely used by nurserymen and fruit growers for weed control among growing plants, but is seldom recommended for this purpose in private gardens mainly because plants differ greatly in their sensitivity to it and an overdose can do a lot of damage. It is most suitable for use in rose beds, since roses, being deep-rooted plants, are unlikely to suffer from a chemical which generally remains in the top inch or so of soil. But even for this purpose simazine should only be used at half the strength recommended for paths and drives and only sufficient should be used to moisten the surface. Once applied, the surface should not be dug, forked or even hoed, as this would break up the film of herbicide which kills emerging seedlings. If weeds do appear – and simazine will not suppress growth from buried roots of strong weeds, such as couch grass, bindweed, dandelions, docks and thistles – these should be dug out with a spud or trowel with as little surface disturbance as possible.

Short sprinkler bar for precise application of fertilisers or herbicides.

Chemical weed control is not very practicable when the soil is densely covered with plants and becomes virtually impossible if a comprehensive system of ground cover is adopted. But, then, even hoeing becomes impracticable and, if the ground cover is not itself effective in suppressing weeds, the only remedy is to remove them one at a time by hand. It is for this reason that it really is important not to plant ground cover until the site has been completely cleaned of persistent weeds.

Fertilisers

Ornamental plants need feeding just as much as those cultivated for food. Mulches of peat, even when regularly renewed, will not meet all their needs; indeed peat itself contains little available plant food, though it enriches soil indirectly by raising its humus content and so encouraging bacteria which help to rot organic matter and liberate locked up minerals. So it must be supplemented by animal manure, rotted vegetable refuse, other waste products, such as old mushroom compost, dried sewage sludge, bone meal, fish meal and meat meal, or with inorganic fertilisers such as sulphate of ammonia, superphosphate of lime and sulphate of potash.

The advantages of organic manures are that they are all fairly slow acting and so are likely to continue to be effective for months rather than weeks, and also that they contain useful trace elements likely to be lacking in the purified inorganic fertilisers. Their drawback is that they vary greatly in quality according to the way in which they have been prepared and stored and that none of them is likely to contain sufficient of one essential plant food – potash. So chemical fertilisers are usually necessary as a supplement to animal manures, garden compost and organic wastes. For this purpose a relatively cheap compound fertiliser, such as National Growmore, will do very well and can be used at 3oz per square yard in spring with perhaps two more applications each of 1–2oz per square yard in early and mid-summer. Just occasionally, on difficult soils that suffer from specific mineral deficiencies, it may be necessary to go beyond this simple routine and make use of more expensive fertilisers which contain essential trace ele-

Making a compost heap takes time and effort but provides an excellent form of fertiliser.

ments, or even, if the soil is very alkaline, to buy chelated chemicals (they are often marketed as sequestrols) which remain effective even under these difficult conditions. These are exceptions which should only be used when it is known they are necessary.

PRUNING

A few plants need to be pruned to keep them in good health; far more are pruned simply to prevent them from taking more room than can be spared or to alter their natural habit in a manner convenient to the gardener.

Roses

Roses provide a good example of the first reason for pruning. It is their nature to produce their best flowers on fairly young growth and even in the wild some of the older wood is constantly dying out, leaving young stems to take over. As this would be an inconvenience and unsightly in the garden, roses are pruned at least once a year, sometimes more frequently if it seems desirable.

The first purpose of this pruning is to get rid of old stems that are producing little or no new growth and also to cut out any stems or parts of stems that appear to be diseased or weak. This can be done at any time in autumn or winter right up till the end of March, but since modern roses often go on flowering until October or even November most gardeners prefer to leave their rose pruning until February or March.

When the old and diseased wood has been removed the rose bushes will probably look much thinner and more manageable than they did before. For shrub roses it is seldom necessary to do much more, but climbers may need to have some of the remaining stems shortened if they are too long to be tied in conveniently to whatever support has been provided for them. Bedding roses also generally benefit from some further shortening of stems, though just how much depends partly on variety and partly on the purpose for which the roses are required. If they are naturally

A typical standard rose before pruning, with thin, much-forked branches.

When pruning ramblers enough shoots are retained to cover the support.

vigorous roses and it is desired to have as many flowers as possible, it will be sufficient to shorten the strong stems by about a third. If they are not very vigorous varieties or it is more important to have a few large blooms than a lot of smaller ones, it may be wise to shorten the best stems to about 6in and other weaker stems to 2 or 3in. Roses hard pruned in this way will produce fewer stems and therefore fewer flowers than lightly pruned roses, but all the strength of the plant will be concentrated on them.

Some roses only flower once each summer, but most bedding roses bloom more or less continuously from June until autumn in a series of flushes. These are known as 'repeat flowering' or 'recurrent' roses and some varieties repeat more rapidly than others. All can be speeded up a little if the earlier flower trusses are cut off directly they fade. They should be cut off just above a young shoot, if one can be seen or, if not, just above a good leaf, since there will be a growth bud where this joins the stem. It does not take long to 'dead-head' roses in this way and it greatly improves the appearance and performance of the repeat-flowering varieties. But there is no point in wasting time on the non-repeat varieties which will not flower again that year whatever one does

to them and some of which, if left alone, will produce highly decorative crops of hips.

Other Shrubs

There are a few other shrubs that benefit from annual pruning, most notably the purple buddleia (*Buddleia davidii* and varieties) and *Hydrangea paniculata.* Both flower best on the current year's growth and, if cut back each March or April to within a foot of ground level or each stem to within a few inches of the main branches, the young growths will be sturdier and the flower heads of superior size. But no such pruning should be applied to the common garden hydrangeas – varieties of *Hydrangea macrophylla* – for these flower from buds on year-old stems and if cut back each spring they will probably not flower at all.

Above: *try to carry out de-heading about once a week, removing blooms as petals drop.* Right: Hydrangea macrophylla mariesii.

Buddleia davidii *before pruning, typical of the shrubs that flower on the current year's stems.*

All the large-flowered clematis benefit from annual pruning. The later flowering kinds, such as purple 'Jackmanii' and 'Jackmanii superba', are best pruned in February when they can be cut back to within a foot or so of ground level. The early (May and June) flowering kinds, of which 'Nelly Moser' is a popular example, are best pruned immediately after flowering; only the side growths should be cut off, each to the pair of growth buds nearest to the main 'vines'.

Evergreens are best pruned in May or June, and most deciduous shrubs in late winter or early spring if they flower after mid-summer, but immediately after flowering if they flower before mid-summer. But for most shrubs regular pruning is not necessary, any cutting that is done being to keep them in place and to preserve their natural beauty by removing badly placed or overcrowded branches.

These long-handled lopping shears with powerful parrot's-bill blades are ideal for heavy pruning.

Trees

This is even more true of trees which are often horribly mutilated by unnecessary or clumsy pruning. The aim should always be to retain the natural branch pattern of the tree and, since with deciduous trees this can most readily be seen in winter, this is the best time to prune them. Never lop branches mid-way, leaving ugly stumps to produce bush-like clusters of new stems. Instead, start by thinning up through the middle of the tree, removing altogether dead or damaged branches and those that are overcrowded. This may well prove sufficient; if it does not and some branches have to be shortened, do so to a point at which another stem grows from them at such an angle as to preserve the shape of the tree. Similar principles apply to evergreen trees, but with these the work is best done in spring.

Unskilled labour should not be used to thin or lop large trees. This is difficult and, at times, dangerous work requiring the use of special equipment and safety tackle. Specialised firms exist to deal with this kind of work and information can be obtained from the Association of British Tree Surgeons and Arborists, Pembroke Cottage, 11 Wings Road, Upper Hale, Farnham, Surrey.

Wall Shrubs

Perhaps the trickiest problem occurs when normally shrubby plants, such as ceanothus, chaenomeles and pyracantha, are used as wall cover. Their naturally bushy, highly three-dimensional shape has to be altered to a flat, almost two-dimensional shape and this must be done not only without detriment to their health but also without suppressing the flowers or fruits for which they are primarily grown. First a framework of branches must be spread out over the wall and encouraged to go on growing until all the required space is covered. This is largely a matter of training – of tying in young stems quite frequently to wires, trellis or whatever other support has been provided. But concurrently with this, and continuing after the framework of growth has been completed, other stems less well placed, or growing too far forward for convenience, must be shortened or removed. This is best done in summer after the shrubs have flowered and when it can be seen which stems can be removed without cutting off all the berries, if there are any, or without getting rid of all the growth that is likely to flower next year. Many of the side shoots can be shortened to a few inches just as when spur-pruning fruit trees, and badly placed or overcrowded ones can be removed altogether. It is not essential to complete the pruning at one operation. It can be spread over several weeks, more stems being shortened or removed as it becomes clear how much growth is being made and how much can be accommodated.

Right: *tree surgeons may be required to work on large trees like these erect beeches.*

Hedges and Topiary

Many hedges are now made with flowering or fruiting shrubs or with roses and are allowed to grow quite informally. They are pruned with secateurs branch by branch, as seems necessary to preserve an attractive shape and ensure that the whole hedge is well filled with growth. For hedges such as these the general rules of pruning should be followed – the roses having their old stems cut out in winter; early-flowering shrubs, such as evergreen berberis and mahonia, being pruned after flowering, and berry-bearing shrubs, such as deciduous berberis and cotoneaster, being pruned in summer when the position of the berries can be seen and the pruning

Above: *another feature of the Japanese quince is its attractive fruits.*

Right: Berberis Darwinii, *a flowering shrub that makes a handsome hedge.*
Below: *a labour-saving tool, the mechanical hedge-trimmer makes life easier for those with large gardens.*

adjusted to preserve as many as possible.

There is also a renewal of interest in formal hedges and topiary which can give permanent form and pattern to even a tiny garden. In our town garden we surrounded the little vegetable plot with a hedge – or maybe one should call it an edge, for it was very low – of clipped box. This is a very satisfactory shrub for such purposes as it has a dense branching habit, neat foliage and can be kept trim with one or at most two clippings annually – unlike privet which may need clipping every fortnight when it is in full growth.

The best time to give all evergreen hedge shrubs their main trim is in late spring, but they can be clipped at any time from April to September if they are untidy. In small gardens, no doubt, this will be done with shears, but all manner of mechanical hedge trimmers are available which will greatly lighten and speed the work if there is much of it to be done. They are also useful for trimming heathers, helianthemums and lavenders after flowering – all of them apt to get straggly and even to die at the base if not annually pruned in this way. Mechanical trimmers or shears can be operated by cable direct from a mains electrical supply; from a car-type battery (these can be powered from a battery-operated lawn mower); from a lightweight rechargeable battery carried in the handle of the machine, or from a portable generator, which is usually the best method if the garden is large and there is a lot of hedge cutting to be done.

Deciduous hedges such as beech, hornbeam and hawthorn are best pruned in autumn or winter when the sap is not flowing, though if they get untidy a light clipping can be given in summer. Such hedges are generally used as large screens, windbreaks or sturdy outer boundary fences and then tend to develop a lot of tough, fairly thick wood. This may be beyond the capability of small power hedge trimmers, so if mechanical cutting is contemplated it will be wise to choose one of the larger, more powerful models and insist on a demonstration of its capabilities before purchasing.

RENEWAL AND REPLANTING

In general trees and shrubs are planted 'for keeps', though sometimes it may pay to plant too thickly in the first place for a quick result and then thin out later on. Some shrubs transplant well even when quite large, rhododendrons and azaleas being notable examples. But once the required permanent planting balance has been established, transplanting or replacing are likely to be minimal.

It is quite otherwise with annuals, biennials and bedding plants which need annual (or even

more frequent) replacement. The hardy annuals must be re-sown each spring or early autumn where they are to flower, and the half-hardies must be reared under glass in spring for planting out in May or early June when danger of frost is over, or if no facilities exist for home raising they may be purchased then as well-grown seedlings. The biennials – including plants such as wall-flowers and Brompton stocks conveniently treated as such though they may have a potentially longer life – are raised from seed sown outdoors in May and June, the seedlings being transplanted to a nursery bed from which they will again be moved in autumn to the place in which they are to flower the following spring or summer.

Bedding plants – a term which includes such popular, non-stop suppliers of summer colour as pelargoniums (geraniums), dahlias and fuchsias – are such a miscellaneous lot that it is impossible to generalise about them. Each must be treated according to its needs, renewed from seeds, cuttings or division, protected in winter or discarded in autumn and replaced the following spring or early summer.

Some bulbs also have this need for frequent renewal or change of soil. Daffodils (a name synonymous with narcissus) can be left undisturbed for years, which makes them excellent for naturalising in grass, and the same applies to crocus and snowdrops. Tulips and hyacinths do better if they are lifted each summer as soon as their foliage dies down, stored in a dry, cool place until September and then replanted.

There are other bulbs or corms – which, from the gardener's point of view, comes to very much the same thing – that are too tender to be left outdoors but can be stored dry in any frost-proof place and planted out in April when the weather is getting milder. Gladioli are the most important example of this.

Lilies, though bulbous-rooted, do not need to be disturbed; they are best planted permanently

Left: *massed daffodils, excellent for naturalising in grass.*

Below: Lilium regale *appreciates being left undisturbed.*

among low-growing shrubs or perennials which will shade their roots but allow their stems to grow up into the sunshine. Only a few, like the martagons, really enjoy shade all the time. Each spring they can be mulched generously with peat or leaf mould, which they love and which, with a little bone meal scattered over the soil at the same time, will help to prevent them from dwindling away as some varieties can do only too readily in gardens.

All this removal and renewal gives a chance for weeds to secure a foothold and so regular soil cultivation must be practised, as in the vegetable garden. Each time plants are removed the soil must be forked or dug so that all weeds can be removed. At the same time it may need to be fed, with manure or compost supplemented with fertilisers, such as bonemeal, which can be specially beneficial to bulbs. There are a few plants one must be careful not to overfeed; pelargoniums, in particular, can grow fat and lazy on too rich a diet, producing lush growth of foliage and few flowers.

Herbaceous perennials, like bedding plants, are such a mixed lot that it can be misleading to generalise about them. Some, such as lupins and delphiniums, are so short-lived that it is wise to renew at least a third of the stock each year, so that nothing need be kept beyond its third year. Others, such as peonies, Christmas roses and Japanese anemones, so dislike disturbance that they are best left alone for five or ten years until declining vigour indicates that they have ex-

Right: *capsicum, better known as red or green pepper, and* below, *the uncommon Swiss chard, both vegetables with attractive fruit and leaves mingle happily in beds and border.*

hausted the soil and must be dug up and given a fresh start. There are yet others, such as Michaelmas daisies, shasta daisies (*Chrysanthemum maximum*), golden rod and heleniums, which grow so fast that they literally starve themselves out, so that only the outer portions of the great clumps go on growing and the inner core dies out. Long before that happens they should be dug up, split into many pieces and only a few of the best outer portions replanted to start the process all over again. Most of this work is best done in the spring, but the beautiful May and June flowering irises transplant well immediately after flowering and repay such attention every second or third year.

FRUIT AND VEGETABLES

It may seem slightly perverse that fruit and vegetables were only included in our town garden, but this was because it was the only one of the three into which they fitted quite naturally. At one stage we did discuss the possibility of making a real French-style *potager* – a garden in which fruit and vegetables dictated the pattern and flowers played a minor role. It is still something that I would like to do because it would be delightful as well as useful, but it would almost certainly be a garden based on rectangles, as our town garden was, for that is the form into which fruit and vegetables fit most comfortably. Most need to be in straight rows for ease of management and, though a few vegetables – such as runner beans (to cover walls and fences), cardoons, globe artichokes, variegated cabbages and kales, sweet corn and numerous herbs – can be mixed in with the more permanent ornamental plants, most of them should be in plots

Right: *broad bands of colour, interspersed with cobble 'beaches', edged the pool to the suburban garden. All too often haphazard arrangements of too many small, bright plants, overwhelm the integral design pattern.*
Left: *the summer pruning of redcurrant consists of shortening all laterals back to five leaves.*

that can be cleared, cleaned and resown or replanted according to the seasonal requirements of the crop.

If the vegetable plot is only to be used for specialities (and that was our intention in the little town garden) it really does not matter how small it is. But, if it is to be used to supply the major seasonal requirements of a family, it will need to be of fair size, at least 300sq yd for two adults and two children and up to $\frac{1}{4}$ acre if a year-round supply of potatoes is to be included, plus plenty of surplus peas, beans, broccoli, etc, to be deep frozen for out-of-season use. When vegetable gardens grow to that size it will be wise to consider the possibility of mechanical cultivation. If one of the small rotor-driven cultivators is used – and these are the most readily manoeuvrable in awkward places – it will be wise to think in terms of plots at least 20ft wide; while for a wheel- and rotor-driven machine – a type less tiring to handle – even wider beds will be desirable to cut down the number of turns that have to be made. There should also be good paths to permit the machine to be swung round easily and, of course, no obstructions or low overhanging branches to get in its way.

Trained fruit trees have obvious advantages in gardens, since they can be kept strictly in place and can fit in very well with the conception of a geometric layout in which they form the major lines of the design – as the French do so brilliantly in their *potagers*. We tried to show, however, that freer, more natural forms, such as the standard or half-standard, can be used decoratively even in a small garden. If other plants or vegetables are grown beneath the fruit trees, serious problems may arise when spraying becomes necessary, since what is good for the trees may be very bad for the plants beneath; so we surfaced the soil beneath the three standard apple trees in our town garden with loose gravel. This would in no way impede feeding them with fertilisers, would make it easy to approach them at any season for pruning, picking, etc, and would almost completely overcome the spraying problem. If a pool were nearby it would be necessary to cover the adjacent section of water with polythene to protect any fish when spraying the fruit trees with derris or certain other insecticides. In fact we did not put any fish into our pool, which was intended primarily as a smooth mirror surface to the sky, and this would almost certainly be the best policy whenever water is used very close to fruit trees.

Standard, half-standard and bush fruit trees are pruned mainly in winter; the work consists

After planting, cut raspberries down to 9–12in. With established plants, cut out the old canes when fruiting finishes.

When pruning young apple or pear bush trees, aim at building an open-centred bush with equally spaced branches.

With established trees, do only essential branch thinning and so encourage fruit buds to develop.

principally of preventing branch overcrowding and providing new stems to take the place of older branches as they cease to be profitable. By contrast most of the pruning of trained trees is done in summer since its purpose is to restrict growth. One way of doing this is to deprive the tree of quite a lot of its foliage after the critical May–June period, when young fruits are beginning to swell and next year's fruit buds are being formed, but before a lot of food manufactured in the leaves passes back to the roots to stimulate their growth. It is work that is best done little by little between mid-summer and mid-August and, since it necessitates frequent close examination of the trees, it is desirable to have them near paths or flanked by grass walks which will facilitate access. In our town garden we adopted the first of these alternatives for the line of cordon apple trees that formed the right-hand boundary as viewed from the house.

Opposite
Top: *foreground planting of the suburban garden was of hostas and* Viburnum opulus *'Sterile' (snowball tree).* Bottom: *ground cover planting of the variegated dead nettle* (Lamium galeobdolon variegatum). *An attractive plant in winter but invasive unless controlled.*

In country gardens the probability of serious seasonal attacks by birds must also be considered. In cold winters green crops can be stripped in a day; in spring, seedlings may be pulled out in thousands in a search for insects; peas, beans, strawberries, raspberries and cherries are taken before they are ready for harvesting, and in autumn it is the turn of the ripening apples and pears to be pecked. Bird scarers and bird deterrents may have some effect, but the only sure method of preserving all crops is to enclose them in a bird-proof cage. When these cages were made with galvanised wire netting they were cumbersome and costly; in the modern garden thin nylon netting is used just as effectively and with much greater economy and comfort.

PESTS AND DISEASES

No garden can remain entirely pest- and disease-free any more than it can be kept entirely clear of weeds. Fortunately, in the highly mixed population of most pleasure gardens, pests and diseases are much less menacing than they are in the block culture characteristic of market gardens and orchards. A great many ornamental plants never need any spraying at all and the same is true of most vegetables. Even fruit trees in the private garden benefit from the mixed population of plants around them, some of which harbour natural predators which keep to tolerable levels the insects and other small creatures feeding on plants.

All the same there will be occasions when these natural measures of control are insufficient.

The only sure way of protecting fruit crops is to enclose them in a bird-proof cage like this one.

Some of the highly bred families of ornamental plants, such as roses, chrysanthemums, dahlias, fuchsias and lilies, are liable to swift attack by sap-sucking aphids (greenflies, blackflies etc), capsid bugs and other pests, if the weather is favourable to them. Some rose varieties are very susceptible to black spot or mildew, and chrysanthemums have a mildew of their own which can be crippling in the autumn. In the vegetable garden, broad beans are sometimes severely checked by blackfly just as they are starting to flower. Cabbage moths and cabbage butterflies can lay so many eggs on brassica crops around mid-summer that the leaves are skeletonised by the resultant caterpillars almost before one realises what is happening, and a little later in the season maturing potatoes and tomatoes can be reduced to blackened pulp by blight.

Some apples, the delicious 'Cox's Orange Pippin' prominently among them, rarely escape a disfiguring disease known as scab; strawberries may be made inedible by grey mould, and raspberry fruits may become the home of maggots of the raspberry beetle.

Fortunately a very few remedies will suffice to give reasonable control of all these ills. Derris and pyrethrum are safe insecticides that can be used to kill caterpillars, aphids and maggots on vegetables and fruit. Since both work only by

Right: *Chrysanthemum 'Westfield Bronze'. Some chrysanthemums are attacked by aphids.*

being brought into direct contact with the insects it is useless to apply them until the pests appear or are known to be about.

Systemic insecticides, such as menazon, dimethoate and formothion, do not suffer this limitation since they enter into the sap of the plant, poisoning it in advance against aphids and some other insects. Each can remain effective for upwards of a month, so that three or four applications from about the middle of May to mid-August can suffice to give plants all the protection they require against some of their most common foes. All three of these chemicals have been passed for use on food crops subject to observance of specified time lapses between last application and harvesting. All the same – simply because these chemicals do enter into the plant and therefore cannot be removed by wiping, washing or even by cooking, and because scientists are sometimes wrong in their pronouncements about safety – I prefer not to use systemics on food crops. I have no objection whatsoever to using them on ornamentals and find that by so doing I not only save a lot of time but also get a more certain control of pests.

Systemic fungicides are also available for black spot and mildew and I recommend them strongly for roses. Benomyl (marketed as Benlate) and chloraniformethan (marketed as Milfaron) are two that have given excellent results. But they do not appear to be as long lasting as the systemic insecticides and fortnightly applications from mid-April until mid-September may be required to give complete control.

For diseases of food crops I would again prefer chemicals that remain on the surface and can be readily removed. Captan against apple scab and strawberry grey mould; dinocap against mildews, and a copper fungicide against potato blight are probably as useful a trio of fungicides

The possibilities of a roof garden with greenhouse and container-grown flowers.

as any to keep ready in the garden store cupboard. Potatoes and tomatoes need not be sprayed before July so the early crops need no spraying at all. Three or four fortnightly sprayings of strawberries with captan in May and June should be sufficient to control botrytis, but apples and pears that are very susceptible to scab may need fortnightly spraying from mid-April until mid-September.

Small power-operated spraying machines are available and a sophisticated atomiser, the Turb-air, powered either by petrol (a very noisy machine) or electricity, will make short work of spraying large areas. But spraying is as a rule so relatively small a part of the garden routine that a hand-operated machine is adequate. Personally I favour the simple syringe-type sprayers with their own built-in fluid container, but the most popular machines seem to be the pneumatic models that are pumped up before work commences and are given a few more pumps from time to time as the pressure drops.

CONSERVATORIES AND GREENHOUSES

If a conservatory, greenhouse or other covered place in which the climate is artificially controlled is to form part of the garden scheme it will be necessary to consider several matters right from the outset. Before even deciding on the structure one should be clear what one wants to grow in it. Different types of plant need different temperatures, different degrees of atmospheric moisture and different amounts of light. Tomatoes do not grow well in a vinery nor do cacti associate happily with orchids. This does not mean that only one kind of plant must be grown in a plant house, but that the mixture chosen should be compatible; if it is not, the structure

Right: *a typical example of slatted greenhouse staging.*

should be capable of internal division so that different climates can be maintained.

It is convenient to group plants in four categories according to the temperature ranges most congenial to them. 'Cold house' plants need no artificial heat even in winter, will survive quite a lot of frost and in summer will get along very well in a temperature between 13° and 18°C. 'Cool house' plants require a minimum winter temperature of 7°C and a similar summer range to that of the cold house, which means in practice that most years they are unheated from April to October. 'Intermediate house' plants need a winter minimum of 13°C and a summer range of 16°–21°C, and 'warm house' plants an 18°C winter minimum rising to 21°–27°C in summer. Not only is greater heat required to maintain the higher temperatures but it is needed for much longer periods, which means that warm houses are disproportionately more expensive to run than cool houses.

It will almost certainly save money and be most convenient if the greenhouse or conservatory is attached to the dwelling-house or fairly close to it. It may thus be possible to heat it directly from the domestic system, and also to light it, so that plants can be tended in the evening when days are short.

Since it is far easier to shade a greenhouse than to provide it with a satisfactory substitute for sunlight, it will be wise to site it in a sunny place. Staging at about waist level is convenient for pot plants, though many permanent plants, such as tender climbers and shrubs, succeed better and require far less attention if growing in beds at ground level.

If heating is installed (and it greatly increases the range of plants that can be grown) it will save both time and money if it is thermostatically controlled.

Left: *a capillary watering system composed of sand bench with polythene underlayer to retain water and plastic pots.*

Automatic ventilation can be carried out either by means of pistons containing a fluid which expands when warm, or by electric fans controlled by a thermostat. Perfectionists can carry this automation a stage farther by installing a controlled humidifier which will maintain the correct degree of atmospheric moisture.

Watering is perhaps the most time-consuming job in the greenhouse. Though there is a lot to be said for hand-watering with a can, if one has the time and knowledge to do it properly (and there is no better way of getting to know your plants intimately), it is far better to use an automatic system than to risk irregular or ill-managed watering. There are several systems available: the simplest is the capillary bench in which the plants stand on a bed of sand kept constantly moist, and the most sophisticated the perhaps rather unsightly 'spaghetti tube' in which each plant receives its water from a thin plastic pipe attached to a larger bore supply pipe. Plastic pots are more suitable for capillary benches than are old-fashioned clay pots, but in any case they are so much lighter, more durable and easier to keep clean that I would always recommend their use whatever system of watering is employed.

Some shading is likely to be necessary for most plants in summer, for the temperature of an unshaded house can run up violently in sunny weather even when the ventilators are open. However, shading is only needed on the sunny side – indirect light never does any harm. Roller blinds can be mounted under the rafters or some kind of shading compound can be sprayed on the outside of the glass. One ingenious proprietary mixture becomes clear when wet but is opaque when dry so that it automatically adjusts itself according to the weather.

Permanent plants grow best in soil mixtures, such as the John Innes potting composts, which can be purchased ready for use. Young plants and those that are not going to be kept for more than a year do well in peat composts which have the merit of being light, clean and very easy to handle. But plants in peat composts require feeding earlier and much more frequently than those growing in soil composts.

Many of the plants grown in greenhouses only need protection when there is danger of frost and can be stood or planted outdoors in summer. This can leave the structure free for a quick crop, such as tomatoes, aubergines or capsicums, or it can be filled with temporary annuals if display rather than utility is the aim.

In a conservatory, however, many of the

Left: *an adjustable slatted plastic sunblind.* Below: *green polythene greenhouse blinds provide shade in summer and retain heat in winter.*

plants will probably be permanent, growing directly in soil-level beds, to provide the 'arbour furnished with greenery' which was a feature of our country garden.

WATER

Properly managed, an area of water is one of the lowest-maintenance garden features, which is one reason why we used so much of it in our suburban garden. Where the water is intended solely for its own qualities of reflection, movement and music, the question of weeds and scum can be dealt with by chemicals and filtration, just as they are in a swimming pool. But for pools stocked with plants and fish, chemical cleansing is a tricky business since the difference between the level of algicide necessary to dispose of scum and blanket weed and the level likely to damage plants and fish is so close that only experts will wish to experiment with it.

So if you opt for a stocked pool you will have to allow for the near certainty that eventually scum and weeds will appear. To some extent they can be kept down by a good balance in the stocking. There should be sufficient submerged oxygenating plants, such as water violet (*Hottonia*) and water milfoil (*Myriophyllum*), to keep the water sweet; sufficient fish to eat up the larvae of gnats, mosquitoes etc, and sufficient water lilies or other plants with floating leaves to provide shade and protection for the fish. It is a little unfortunate that water lilies flower best in a very sunny place, whereas blanket weed and other algae are likely to be least troublesome in the shade. This really means that if you want a flowery pool you must accept a little weed along with the ornamental aquatics. If, despite precautions, this weed growth becomes too dense to be

1

2

3

4

5

Stages in making a formal pool:

1 *ensuring levels after excavation;*
2 *placing sand in bottom to cushion plastic liner;*
3 *putting liner in place;*
4 *adjusting liner while filling with water;*
5 *placing edge slabs in position.*

Right: *the finished pool.*

Left: *submerging oxygenating plants in plastic baskets.*
Above: *an established pool makes a decorative garden feature and provides an opportunity for growing unusual water plants.*

tolerated, it is best pulled out with a rake or Canterbury hoe, or skimmed off the surface with a piece of sacking, a fine sieve or a muslin net.

It is almost always best to plant everything in plastic baskets since this makes it much easier to drag them up again when they get overgrown or seem to be in need of fresh soil. There will also be far less soil in the pool to muddy it or cause fouling through the decay of organic matter. For the same reason I would not advise using manure in the compost, but only good quality, rather stiff loam with at most just a peppering of bonemeal to build it up. Peat and leaf-mould should also be kept out of pools.

Where there are no plants or fish, the water can be kept crystal clear by chlorinating it or by adding copper sulphate at about 1oz per 1,000gal. A sufficiently accurate estimate of the number of gallons of water in a pool can be made by measuring its length, width and depth in feet, multiplying the three figures and then multiplying the result by six.

It is, of course, quite possible to divide a pool so that one section is used for plants etc with untreated water and another without plants is kept crystal clear by chlorination or the use of copper sulphate. It is then essential that there is no seepage or overflow of chemically treated water into any part of the pool containing plants or fish (an exchange the opposite way does not matter). So, if such a scheme is adopted – and it surprises me that it is not more widely used – it is advisable for the planted section to be at a slightly higher level.

It is generally preferable to operate fountains, cascades etc by recirculating the water in the pool by means of a pump rather than direct from a mains supply. Mains water is usually chemically treated and may be much colder in summer than the water in the pool; in neither case is this good for plants or fish. In unstocked pools introduction of tap water will dilute or alter the level of chemicals in the water and may necessitate frequent re-treatment if weeds and algae are to remain suppressed.

Index

A

Acknowledgements

Photographs have been supplied by the following: *Amateur Gardening*, Pat Brindley, John Brookes, Robin Corbin, J. E. Downward, *Financial Times*, Arthur Hellyer, Anthony Huxley, Anthony Martin, Harry Smith, Fred Whitsey.